AF530839

SEEING THINGS

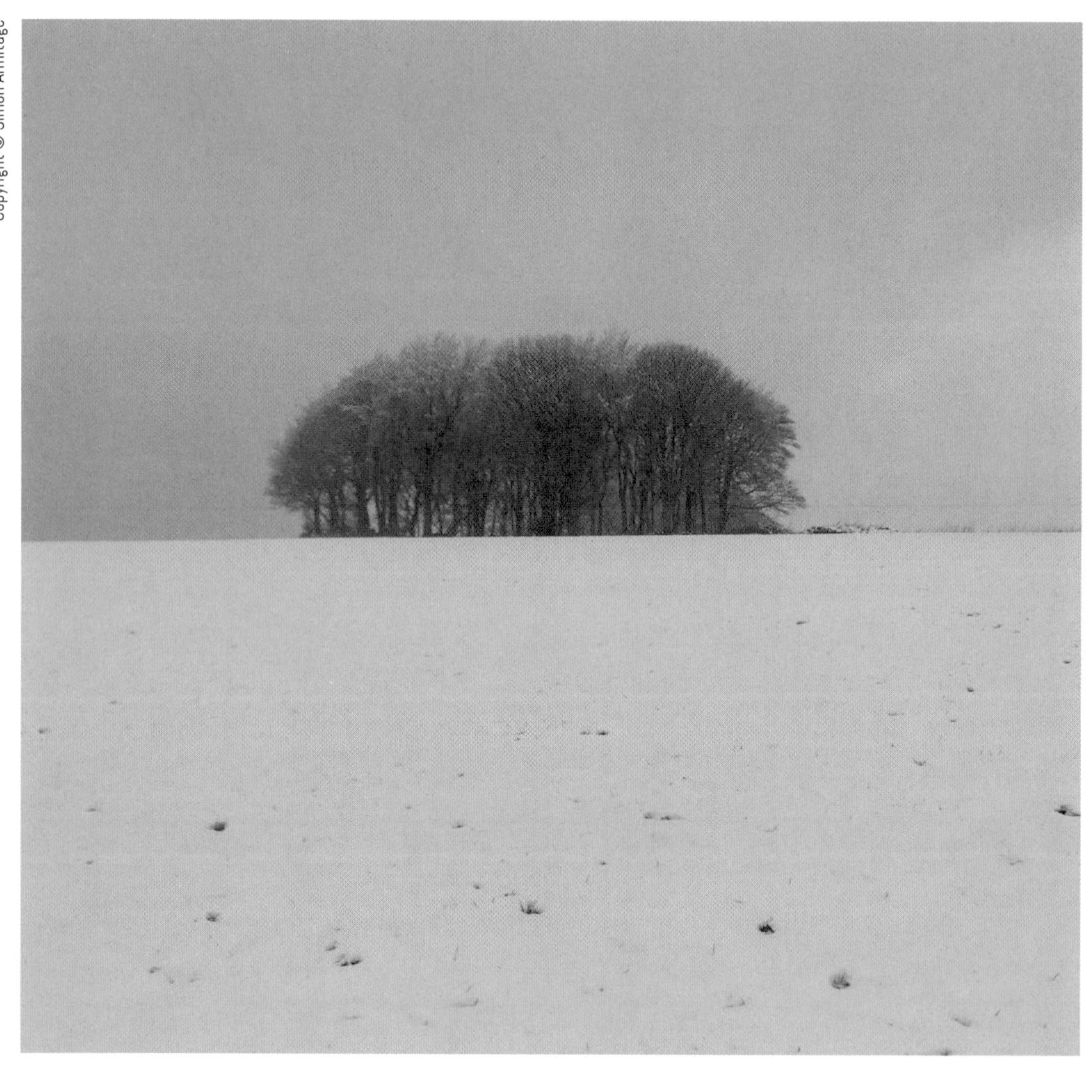

Simon Armitage, Copse.

SEEING THINGS

the small wonders of the world, according to writers, artists and others

EDITED BY JULIAN ROTHENSTEIN

WITH A FOREWORD BY CORNELIA PARKER

AND TEXTS BY CHARLES BOYLE

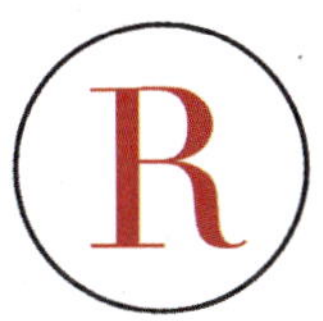

A REDSTONE BOOK

Courtesy Aveek Sen.

PLEASE TAKE YOUR TIME

THERE IS MUCH TO SEE.

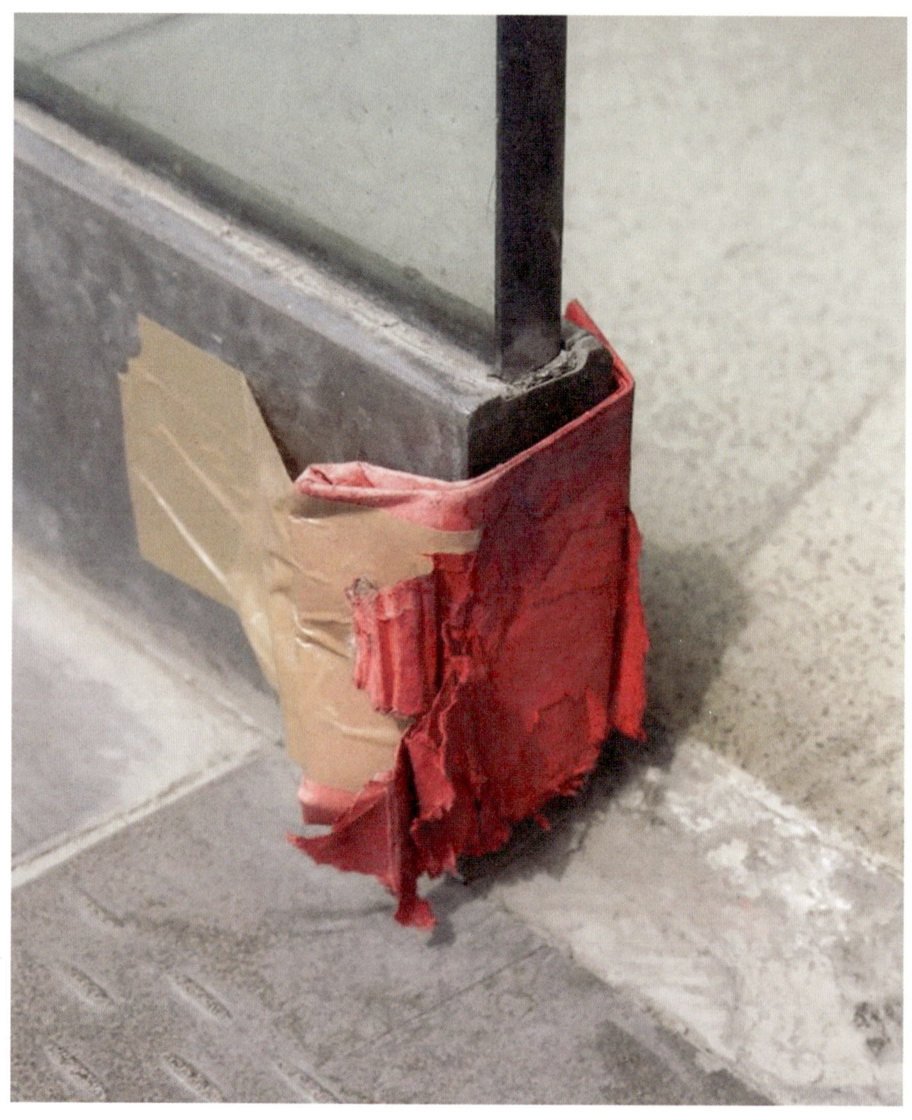

Richard Wentworth, *London, New Oxford Street*, 2015

CORNELIA PARKER
A BRUSH WITH INSTAGRAM

I think artist Richard Wentworth pre-empted the idea of Instagram through his brilliant series of photographs title *Making Do and Getting By* (1974–present). A hugely influential body of work, his images document a surfeit, 'a creativity beyond functionality, a transformative repair'. He has changed the way we look at the world, and stylistically a large number of diverting Instagram images owe a great deal to him, even those made by Instagrammers who don't know his work.

Richard writes: *Put simply, I think my pictures are unremarkable, except in the way that they talk to each other and remind us that humans read the world every time they look. We sense 'intention' and causality in everything we see, the basis for the awful announcements on the Tube for 'reporting anything unusual'.*

I have taken many photographs over the years, using my camera as my sketchbook, as a way of gestating ideas. Some of these images would prompt me to email them to friends, with a line of text or very often just a word. Titling the images helped with the distilling and crystalising of seemingly random thoughts.

When I was invited to be the Election Artist in 2017, I was asked to do some social media, something I had managed to avoid in my life up to then. On the brink of losing my SM innocence, I looked with horror at all the options and chose Instagram, which I then took to immediately. Here was a way to explore disparate ideas, grow an audience of strangers and communicate through images in an instant.

I was told that I couldn't be biased and betray my own political leanings. Initially my reaction was one of dismay, but then I thought: *Actually, this could be really good fun.* Left-Leaning cat, Right-Leaning cat. Left-Leaning Tree, Right-Leaning Tree. Colour coding images in red, blue and yellow in Photoshop. A photo of a US road sign announcing WRONG WAY (white lettering on red background) became WAY WRONG on yellow and MAY WRONG on blue. The over 1,500 posts (photos and videos) I made during my residency, became a three-minute -long animation *Election Abstract* (2018), a documentation of my observations as an investigative reporter out in the field during the campaign. I also made a short film, *Left, Right and Centre,* shot on Saturday night and Sunday morning in the House of Commons with the aid of a drone (both of these can be found on Youtube.)

Since then, I have posted over a thousand more images. A stream of consciousness that helps hone my eye, alerting me to potential wherever I am. It helps generate new ideas for future artworks. It allows me to rail against social injustice, express political views, and visually indulge: the platform provides a fair bit of cat pilates, found abstracts, backs and undersides of objects, and miscellaneous stuff. I might be a late adopter, but I have made up for lost time, and have had the pleasure of meeting many of my followers in person along the way.

NOTE: Texts printed in Bodoni (the serif typeface) are by Charles Boyle. All other captions or texts accompanied the images taken from Instagram.

I: writers and books

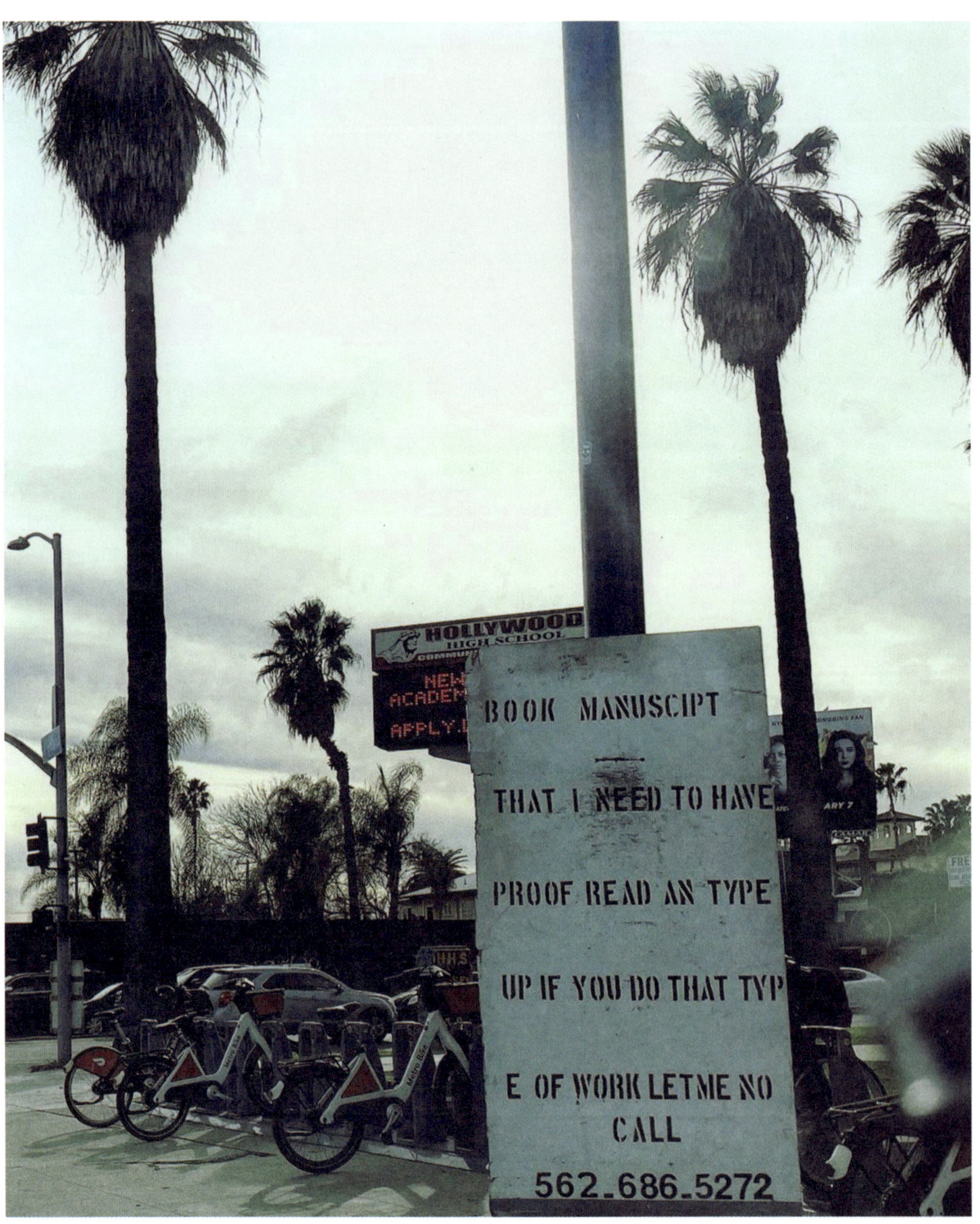
HOLLYWOOD
HIGH SCHOOL
BOOK MANUSCIPT
THAT I NEED TO HAVE
PROOF READ AN TYPE
UP IF YOU DO THAT TYP
E OF WORK LETME NO
CALL
562.686.5272

Relatable.

ANY SCHOOL EXERCISE BOOK from the corner shop will do. No need for a shrink-wrapped one from a twirly carousel. Notebooks are for rough drafts and notes-to-self and play, nothing buffed and polished. A real notebook contains at least three and often more of the following: paragraphs with crossings-out and circles and arrows; isolated phrases meaningless without a context; snatches of talk overheard on public transport; telephone numbers and song titles and film titles and recipes and route directions; lists of names; illegible sentences written when drunk or very tired; cigarette burns, rings from wine glasses, crusty stains of one or another fluid; ripped edges where pages have been torn out; squashed flies, dried flowers, stray hairs; writing in different coloured inks; titles for poems or stories that will never be written; curses, riddles, prayers; sketches of imaginary animals; pasted-in photographs from magazines. A real notebook smells, and not of lavender. A real notebook often has blank pages at the end because all writers at some point, or at recurring points, have dark nights of the soul and want to change their lives and the cheapest way to do this is to start a new notebook.

EDOUARD LEVÉ'S *WORKS* describes 533 works 'conceived of but not realised by its author'. In July 1937, in an application for a Guggenheim Fellowship, James Agee wrote, 'I am working on, or am interested to try, or expect to return to, such projects as the following' – and he listed 47 projects. Among them: 'A story about homosexuality and football' ('an inevitable part of it would be a degree of cleansing the air'), 'A new type of sex book' ('as complete as possible a record and analysis of personal experience from early childhood on, and of everything seen heard, learned or suspected on the subject'), 'A study in the pathology of "laziness"' ('A story of cumulative horror'), 'Analyses of miscommunication' and 'An autobiographical novel.'

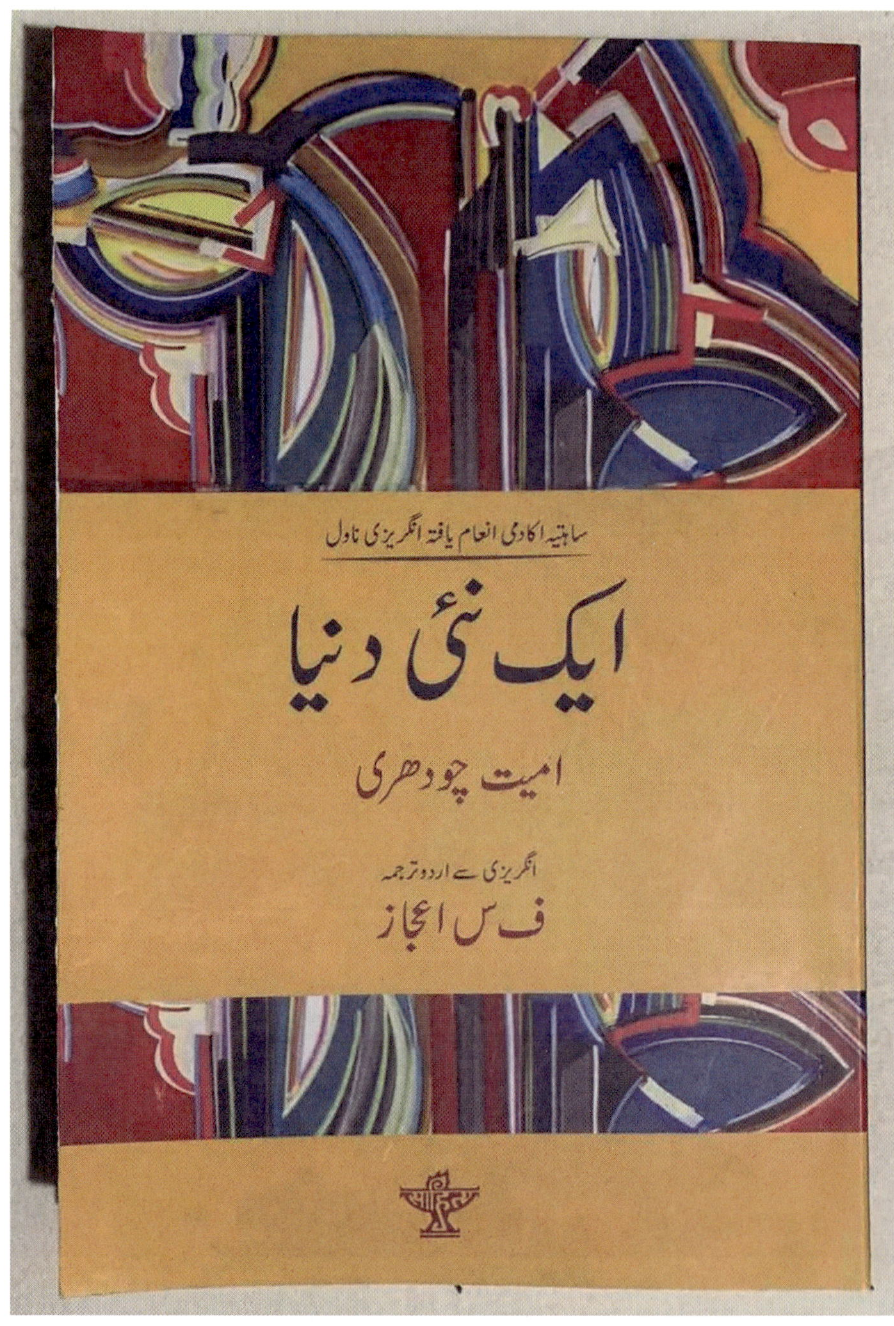

The publication of a book is a strange occasion for the author – a mix of disengagement and nervous anticipation. What happens in the long aftermath is another matter. Receiving copies of the Urdu translation, by Fey Seen Ejaz, of *A New World* from the Sahitya Akademi has given me joy, especially as I wasn't expecting them.

KAMILA SHAMSIE

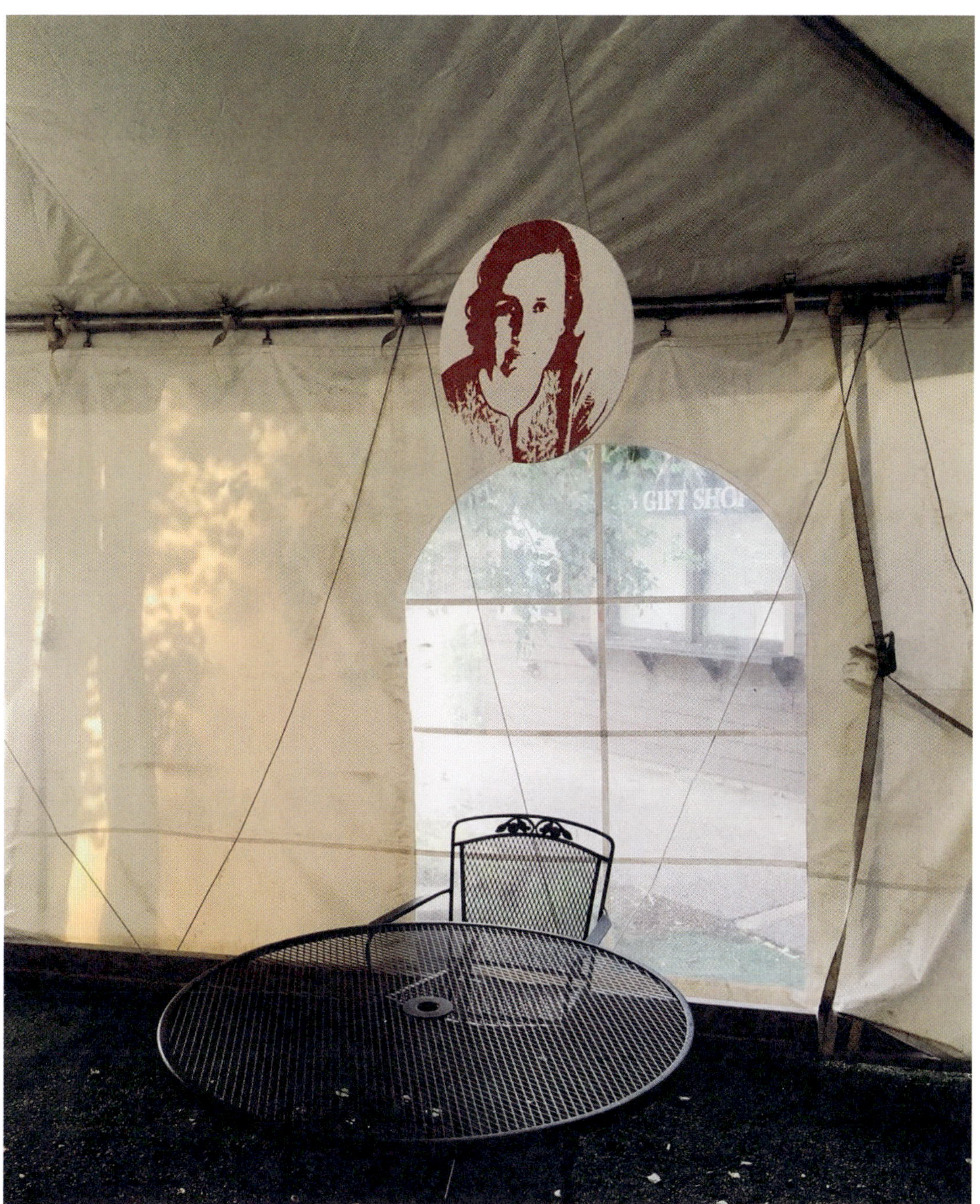

The author as disembodied head.

IMAGINE KNOCKING ON KAFKA'S DOOR. And after half a minute, knocking again, a bit louder. Imagine peering through the letter flap – which Kafka's door almost certainly didn't have – to see what you can see. Hearing footsteps coming down the stairs but no, you're just imagining them. Knocking again, careful not make those knocks sound aggressive, you're not a bailiff, and deciding to wait until ten cars have passed by in the street before giving up and heading home. By the fifth car it has started to rain. You don't have an umbrella. After the tenth car has gone by and Kafka still hasn't materialised, do you (a) quit, go home; or (b) start counting again from one?

ANDREW O'HAGAN

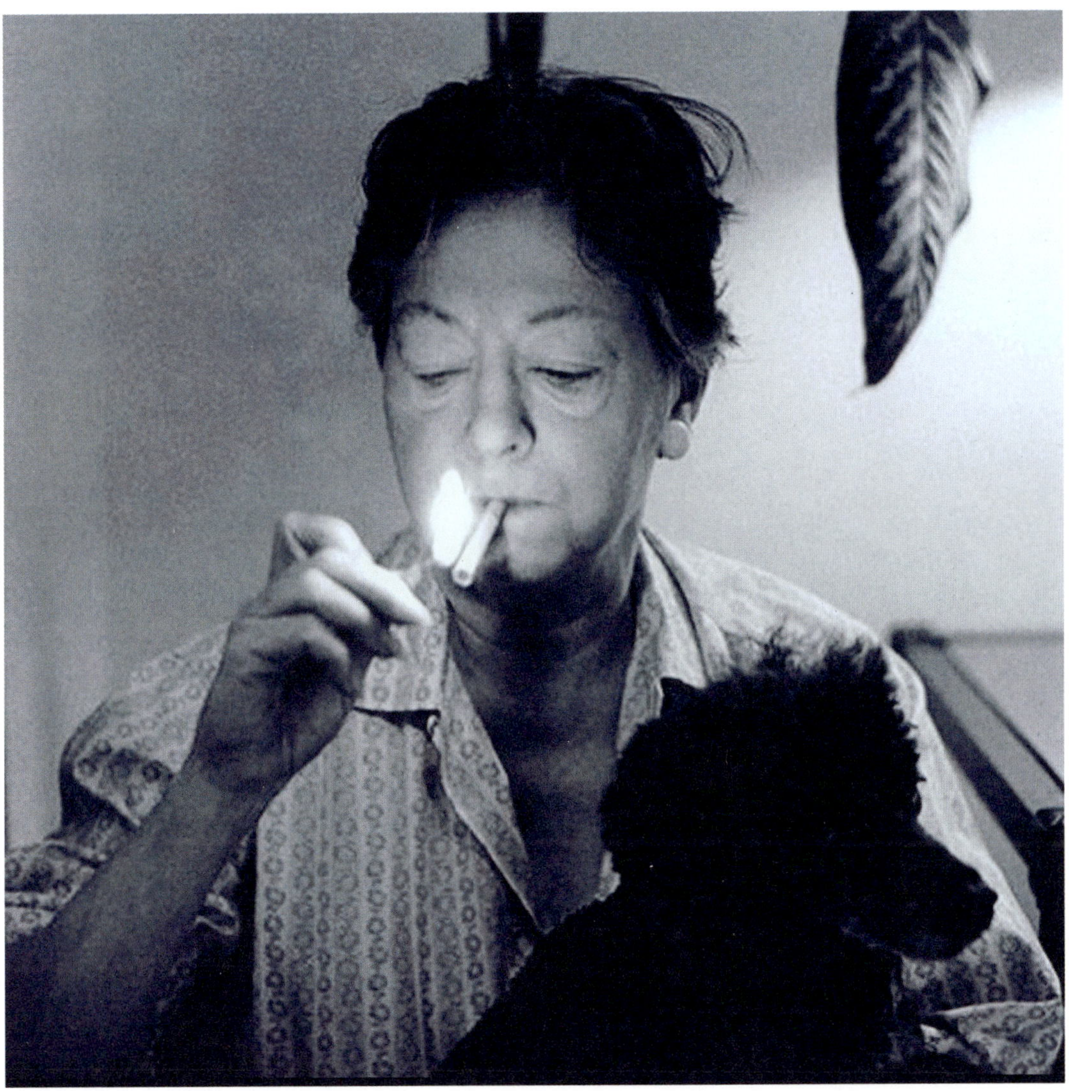

Happy Birthday, Dorothy Parker. 'If you have any young friends who aspire to become writers, the second greatest favour you can do them is to present them with copies of *The Elements of Style*. The first greatest, of course, is to shoot them now, while they're happy.'

ANDREW O'HAGAN

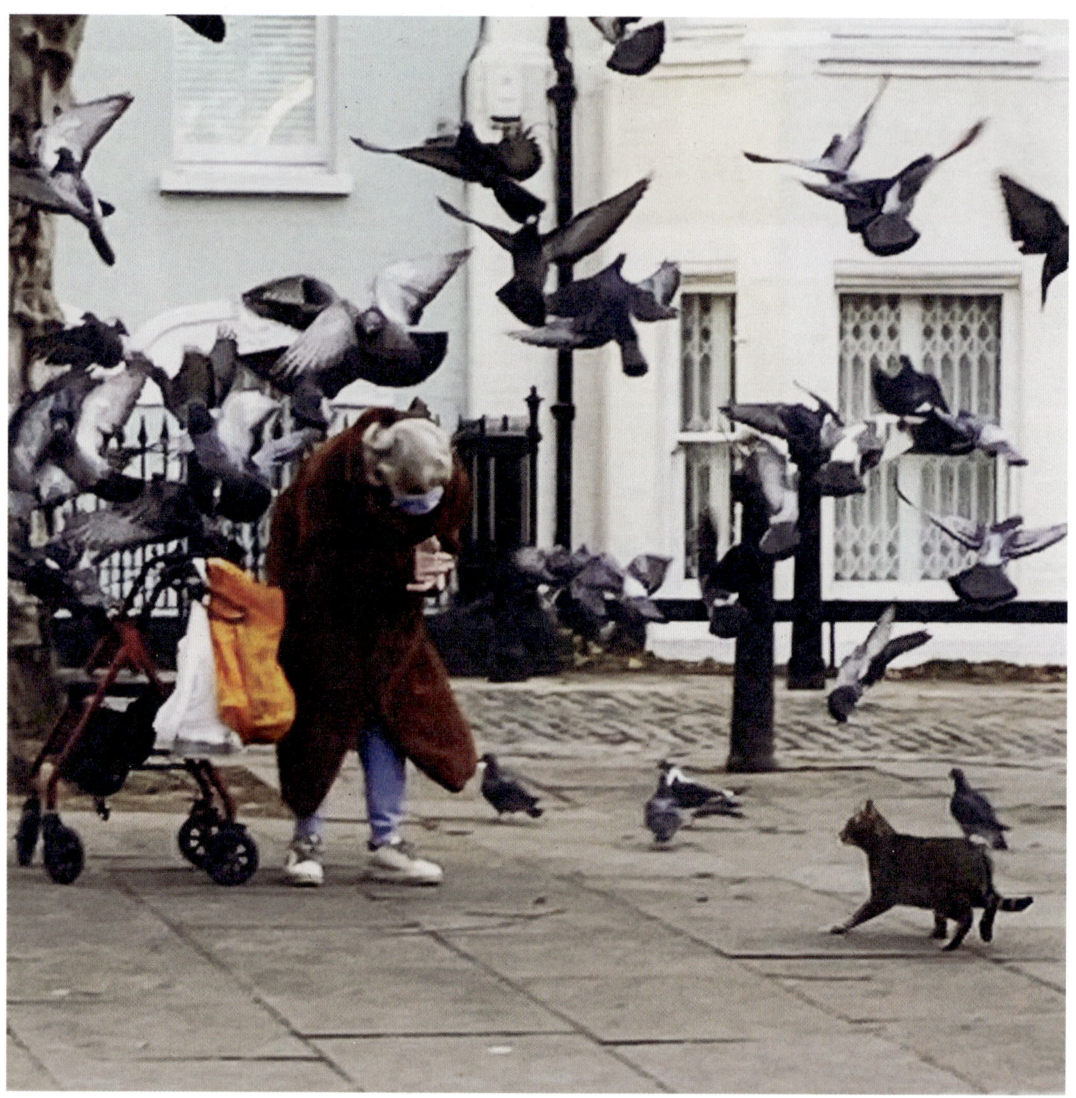

I see this wonderful lady every day. She feeds the birds. Today, she and the cat were among the pigeons, and I just caught it.

ANDREW O'HAGAN

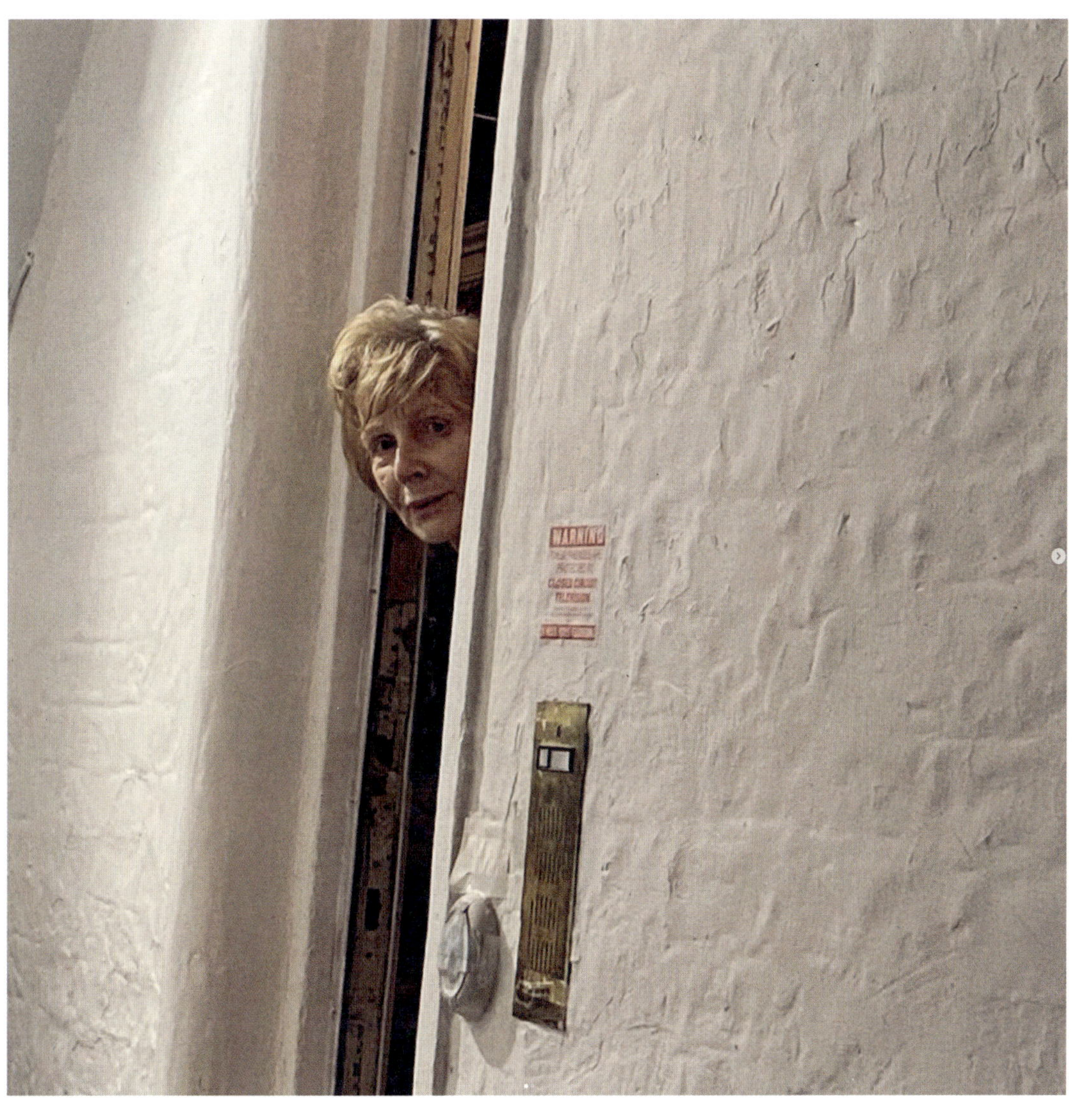

I went over to see Edna O'Brien tonight.

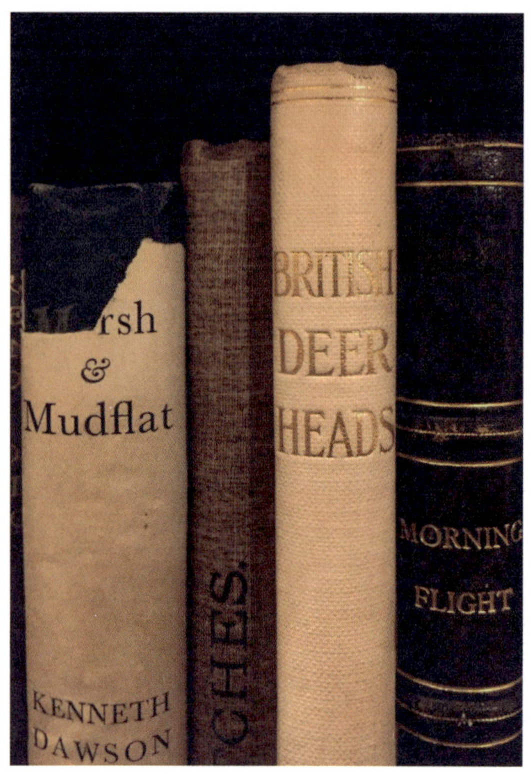

A classic of the national animal parts genre

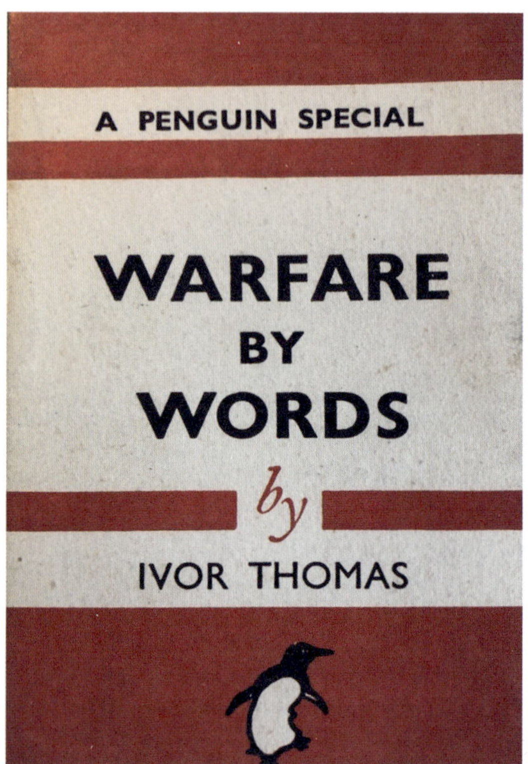

Every day.

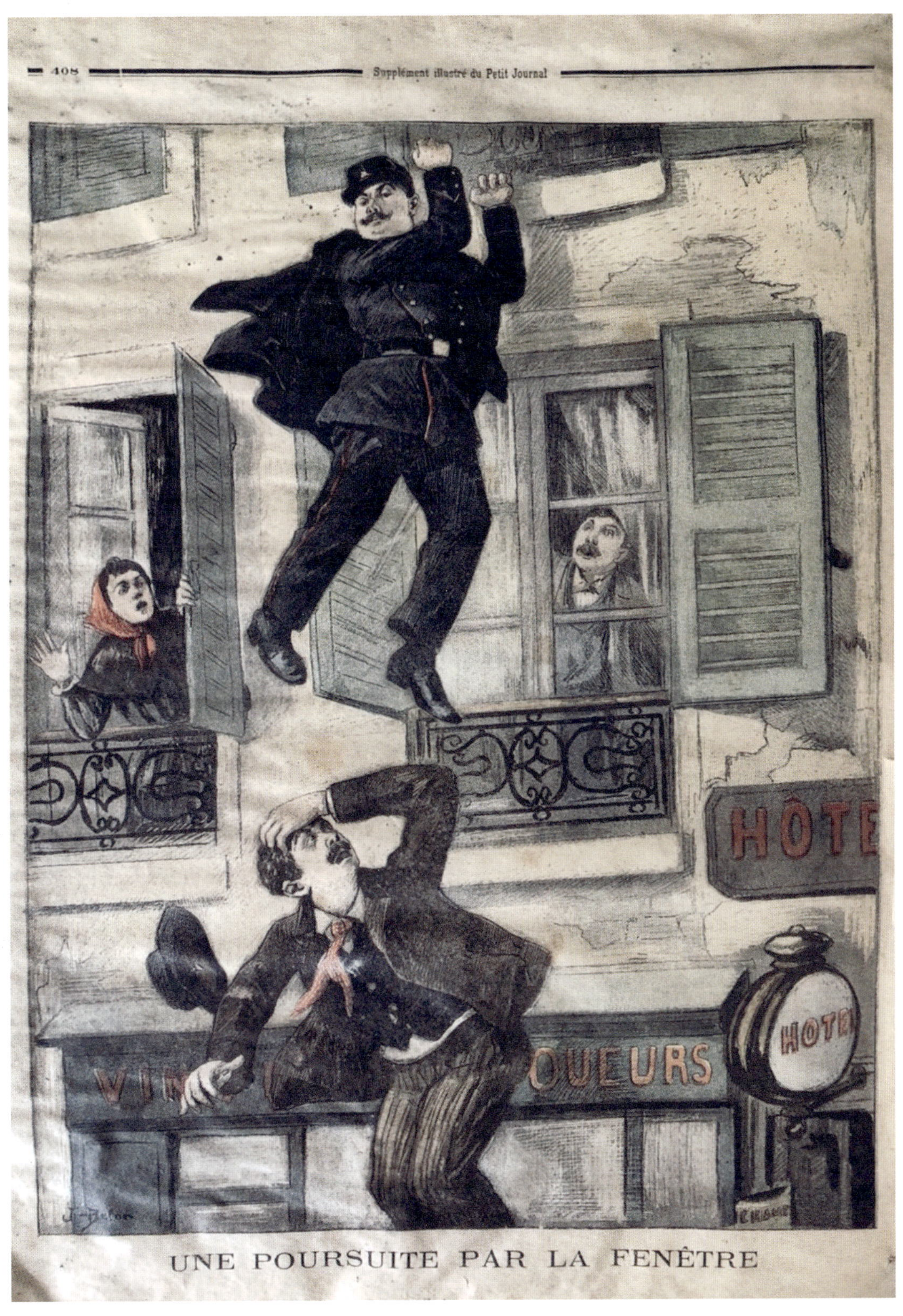

Superhero, 1899.

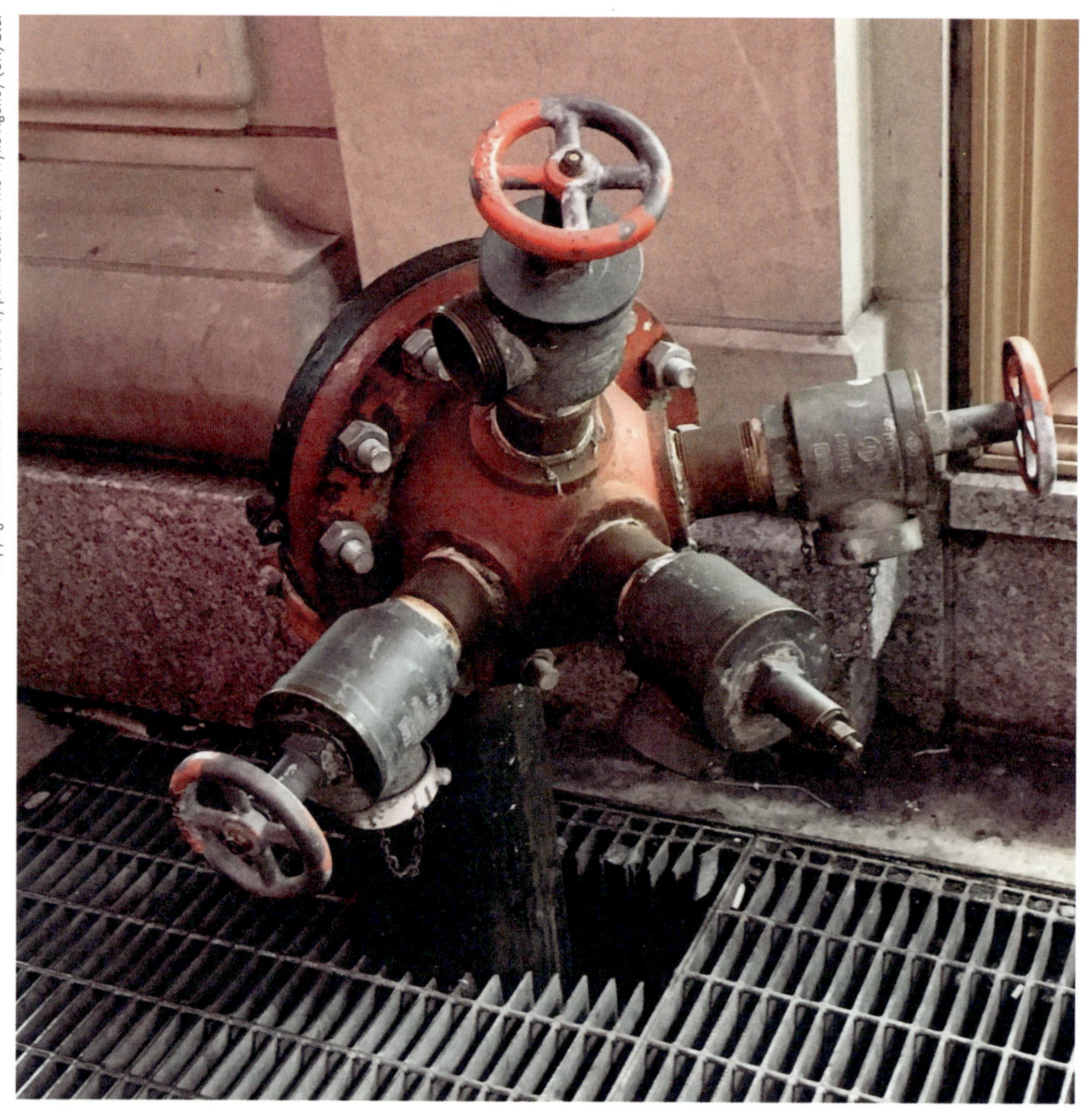

Emerging from the bowels of hell.

ROZ CHAST

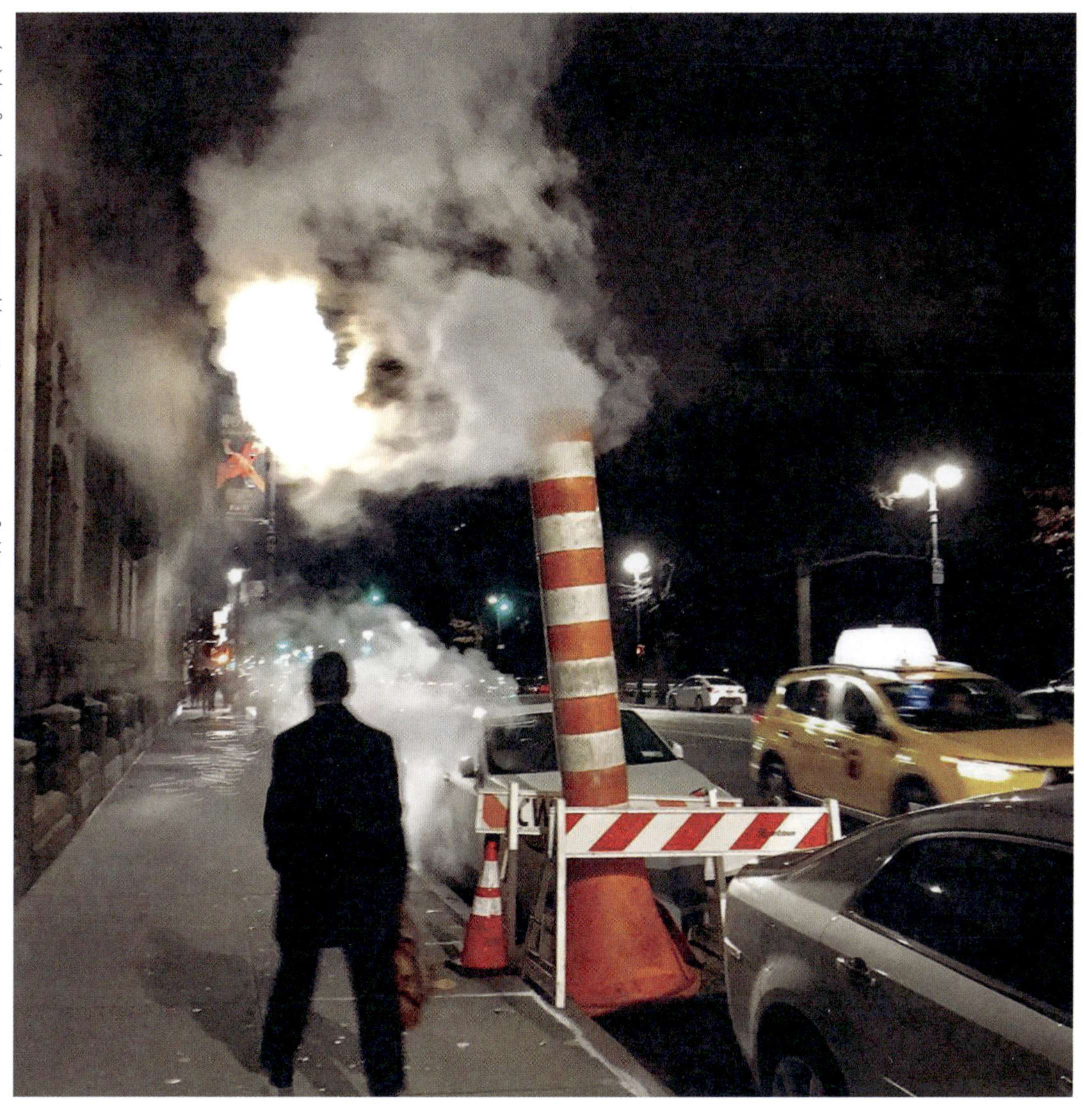

The service entrance to hell.

Tonight the sky looked like
the people in charge of skies
had got a bit carried away.

NEIL GAIMAN

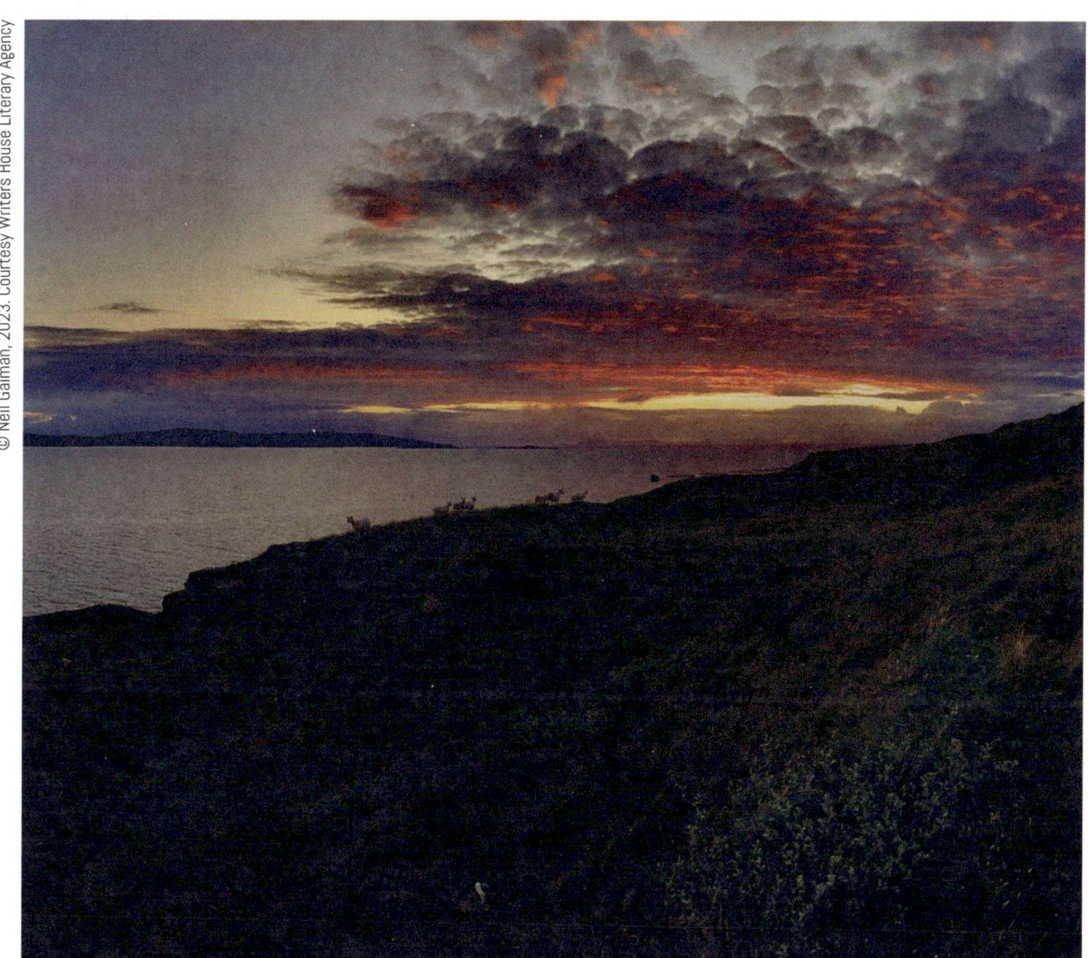

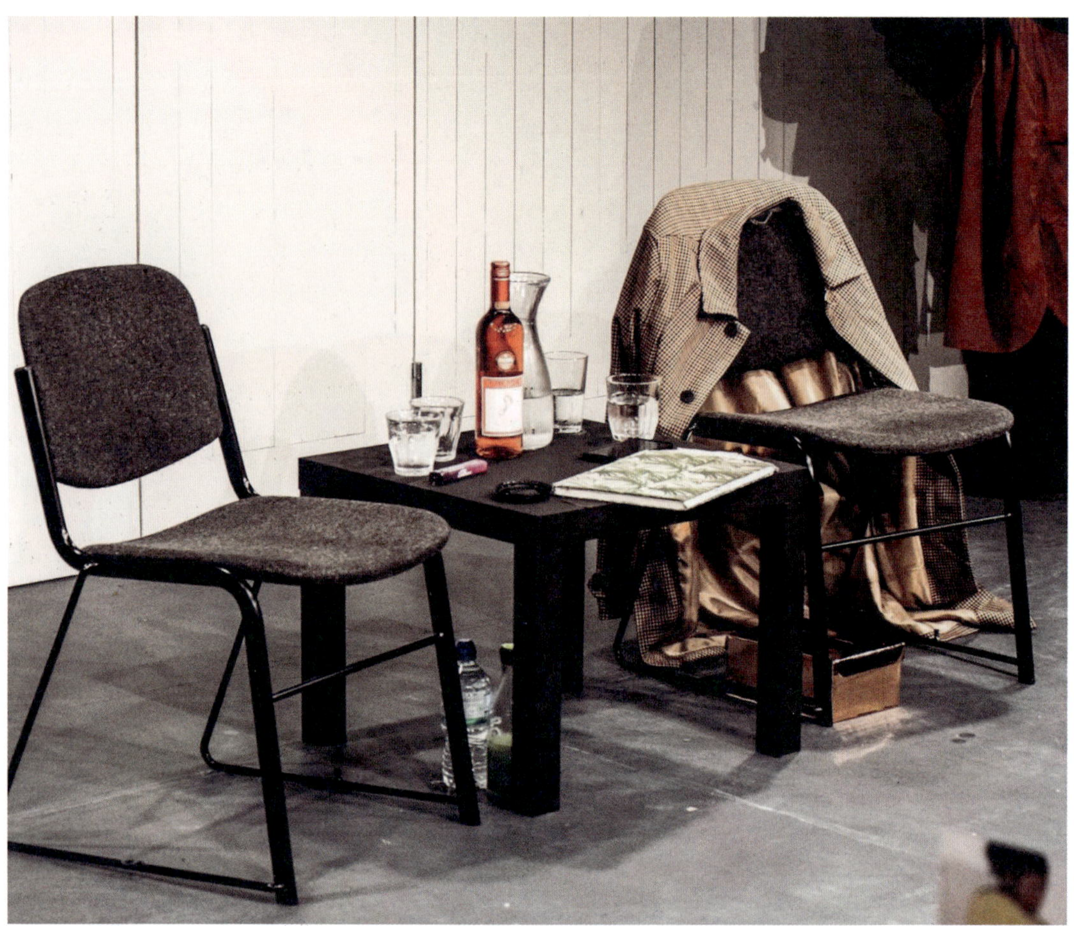

Bush theatre.

KAMILA SHAMSIE

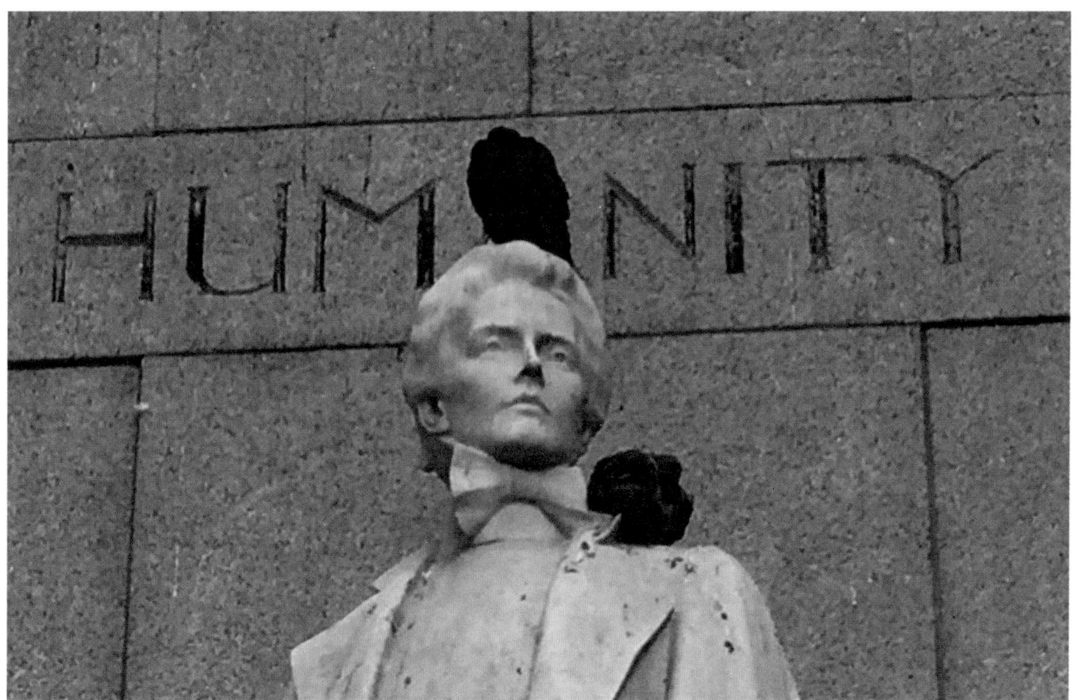

The A in Humanity is a bird.

JOHN GALE: ‘A friend of mine once read *La Chartreuse de Parme* by Stendhal; it inspired him; he determined to change the direction of his life; in the end he just went out and bought himself a new pair of shoes.’

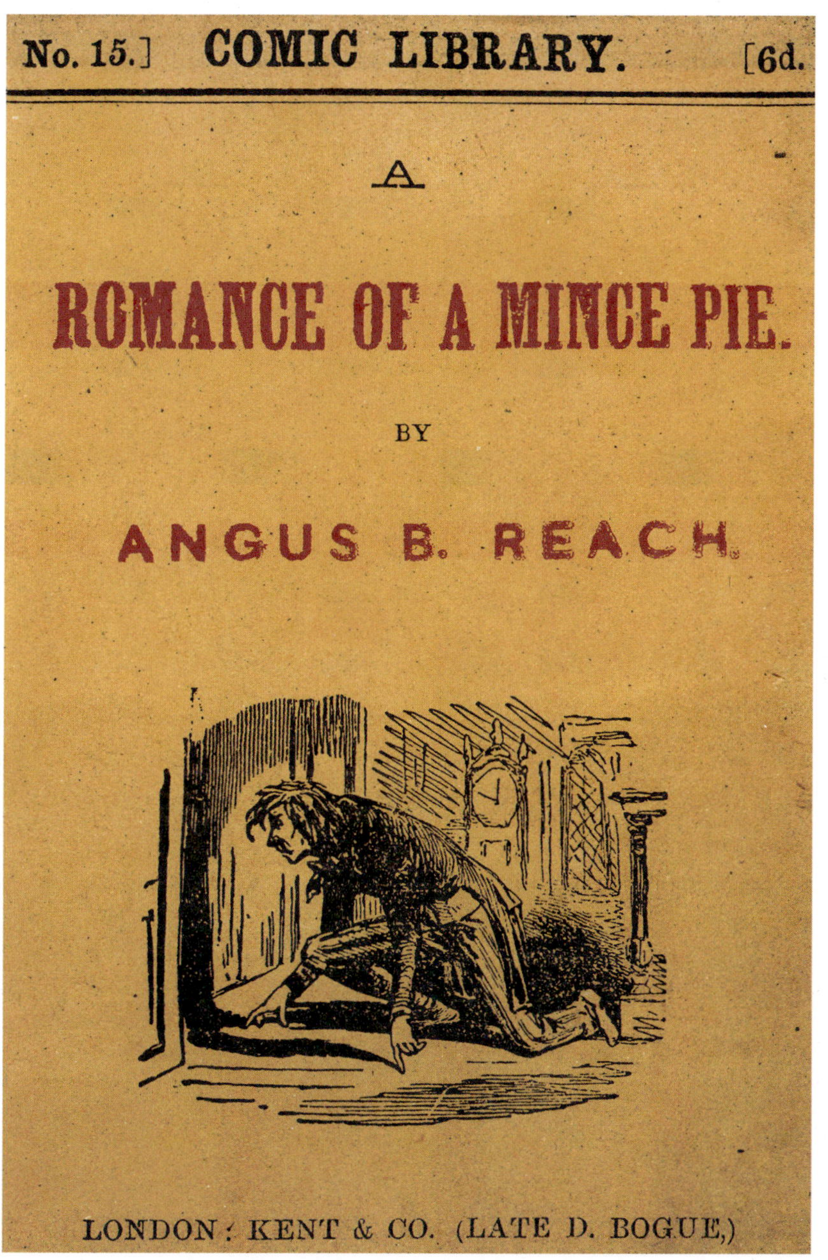

No. 15.] COMIC LIBRARY. [6d.

A

ROMANCE OF A MINCE PIE.

BY

ANGUS B. REACH.

LONDON: KENT & CO. (LATE D. BOGUE,)

Sundays are excellent for catching up with some very important reading.

GARTH GREENWELL

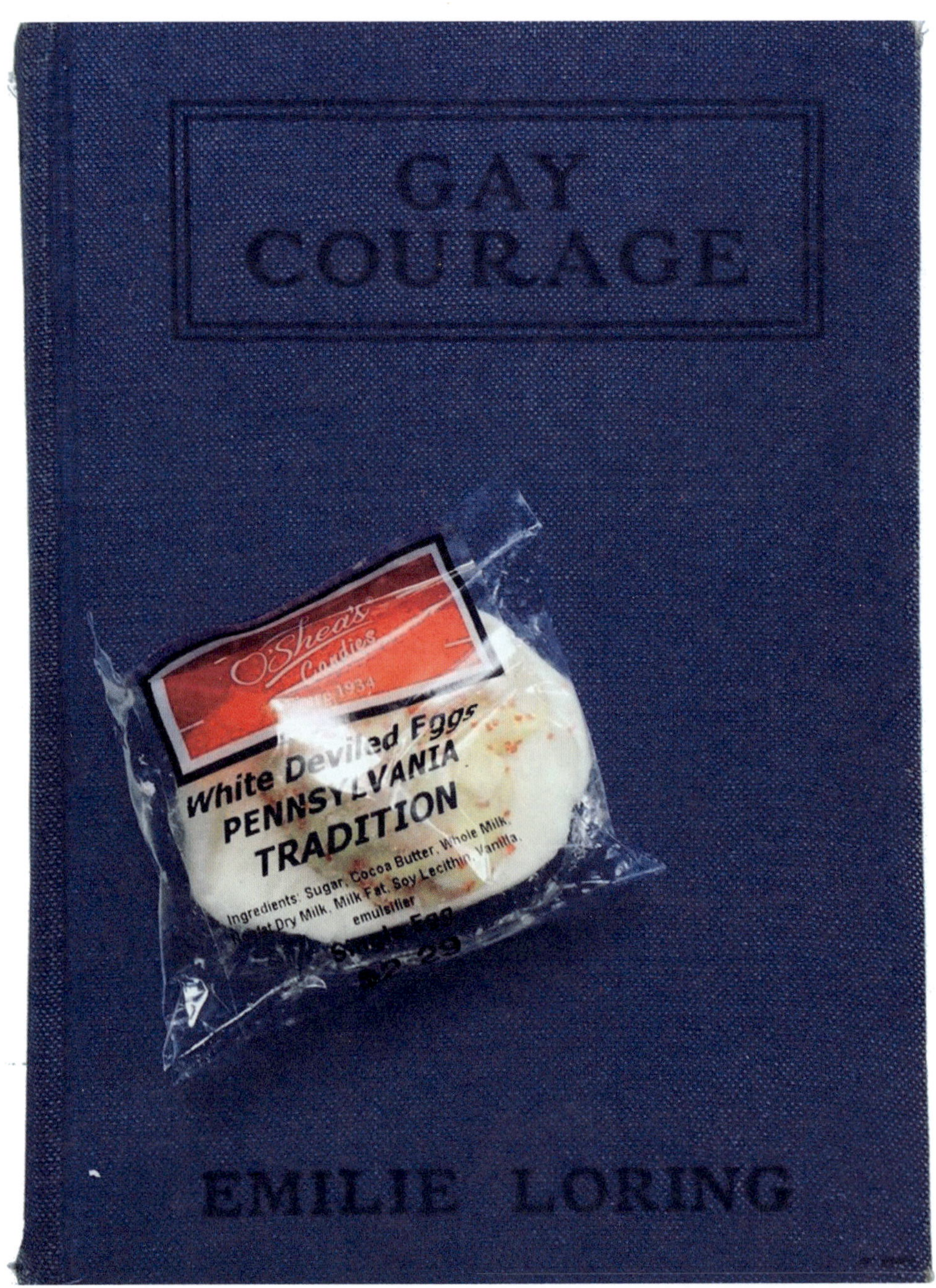

Thank you so much @idranovey for knowing exactly what I need to get through this crisis: novelty chocolate and gay courage.

KAMILA SHAMSIE

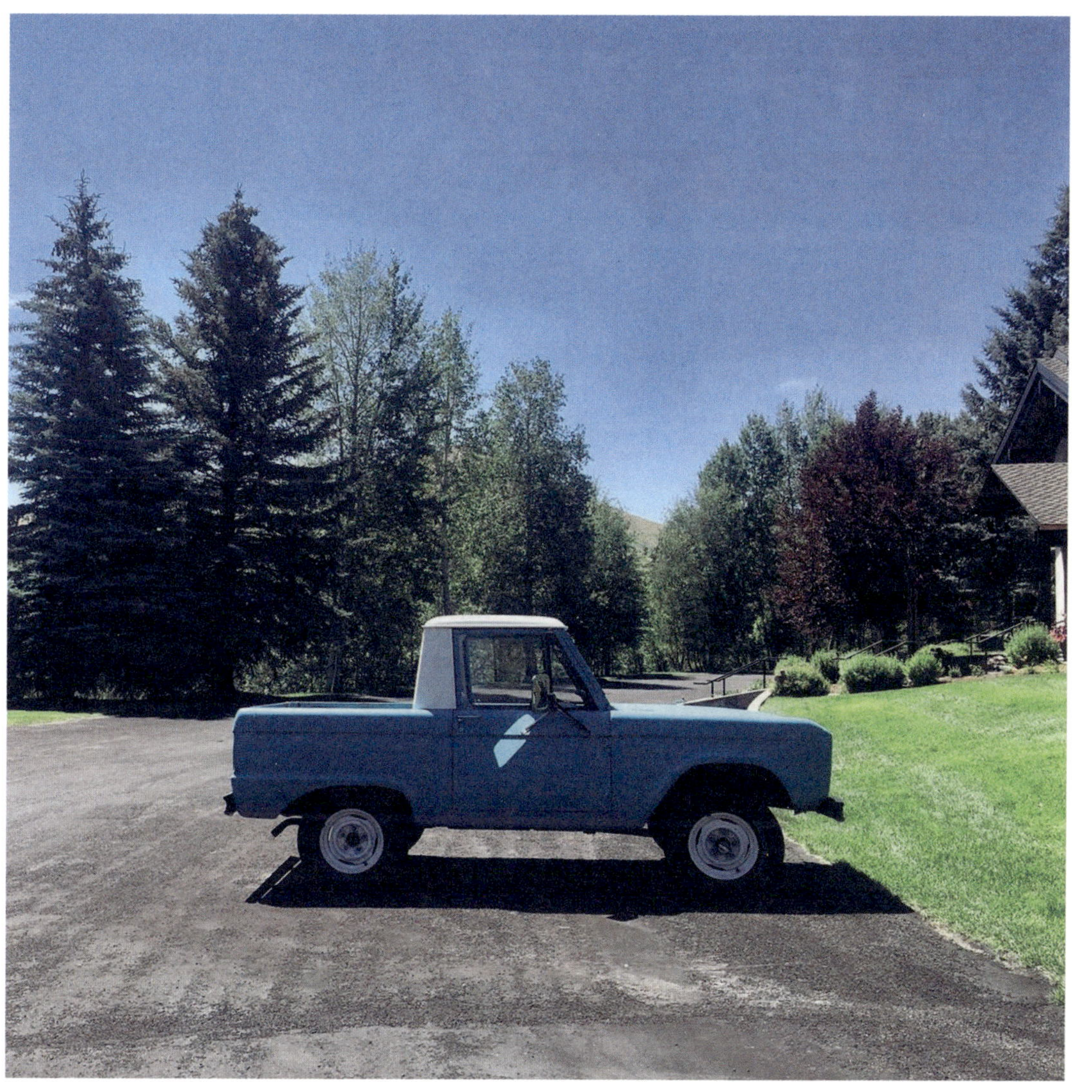

I slightly fell in love with this pick-up.

Probably not a good present to give
a recovering coke-addict.

JARVIS COCKER

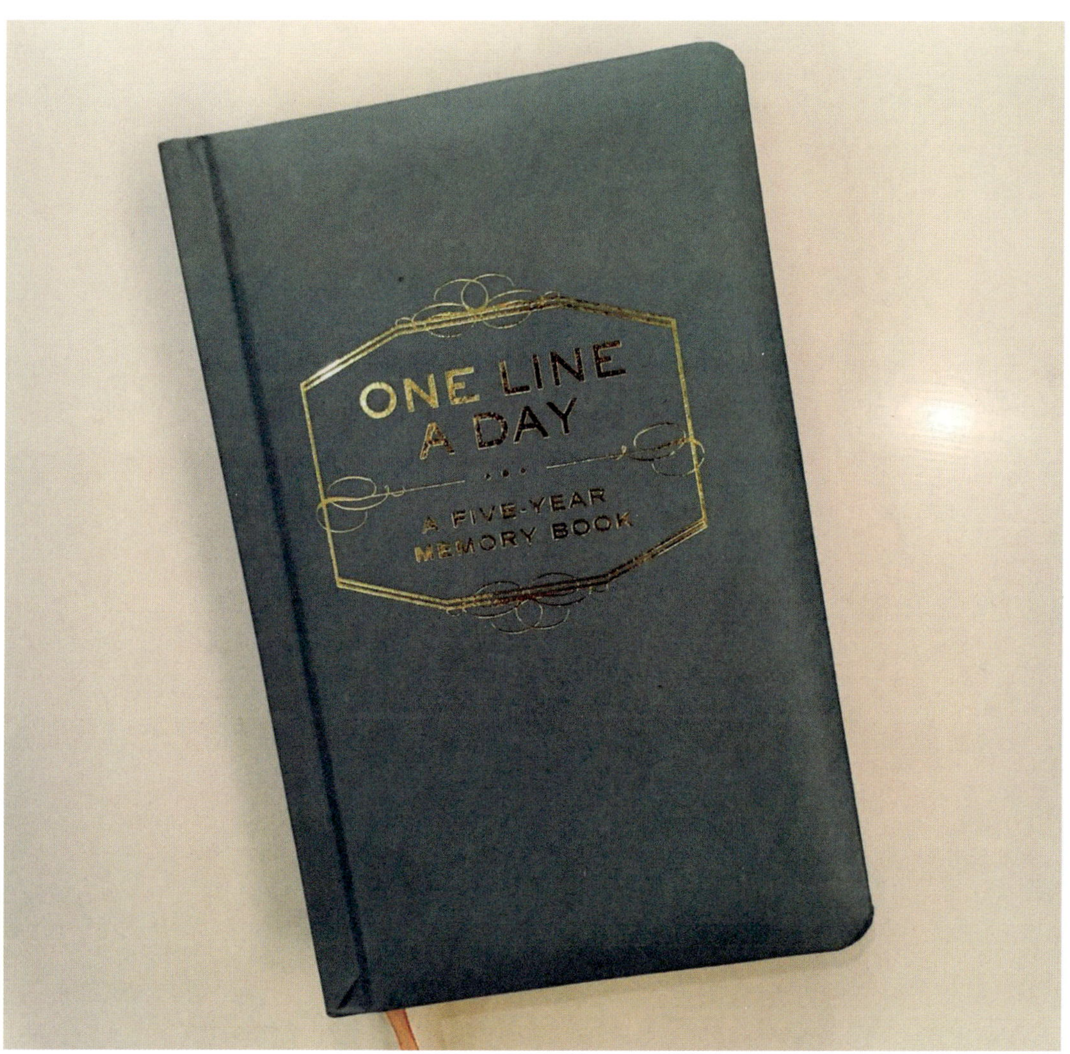

NO
THANKS
TO
Farrar & Rinehart
Simon & Schuster
Coward-McCann
Limited Editions
Harcourt, Brace
Random House
Equinox Press
Smith & Haas
Viking Press
Knopf
Dutton
Harper's
Scribner's
Covici-Friede

I love that e e cummings, when nobody would publish his work, self-published it under the title *No Thanks*, with the help of his mum – and the dedication is to the fourteen publishing houses who turned the collection down. IN THE SHAPE OF AN URN.

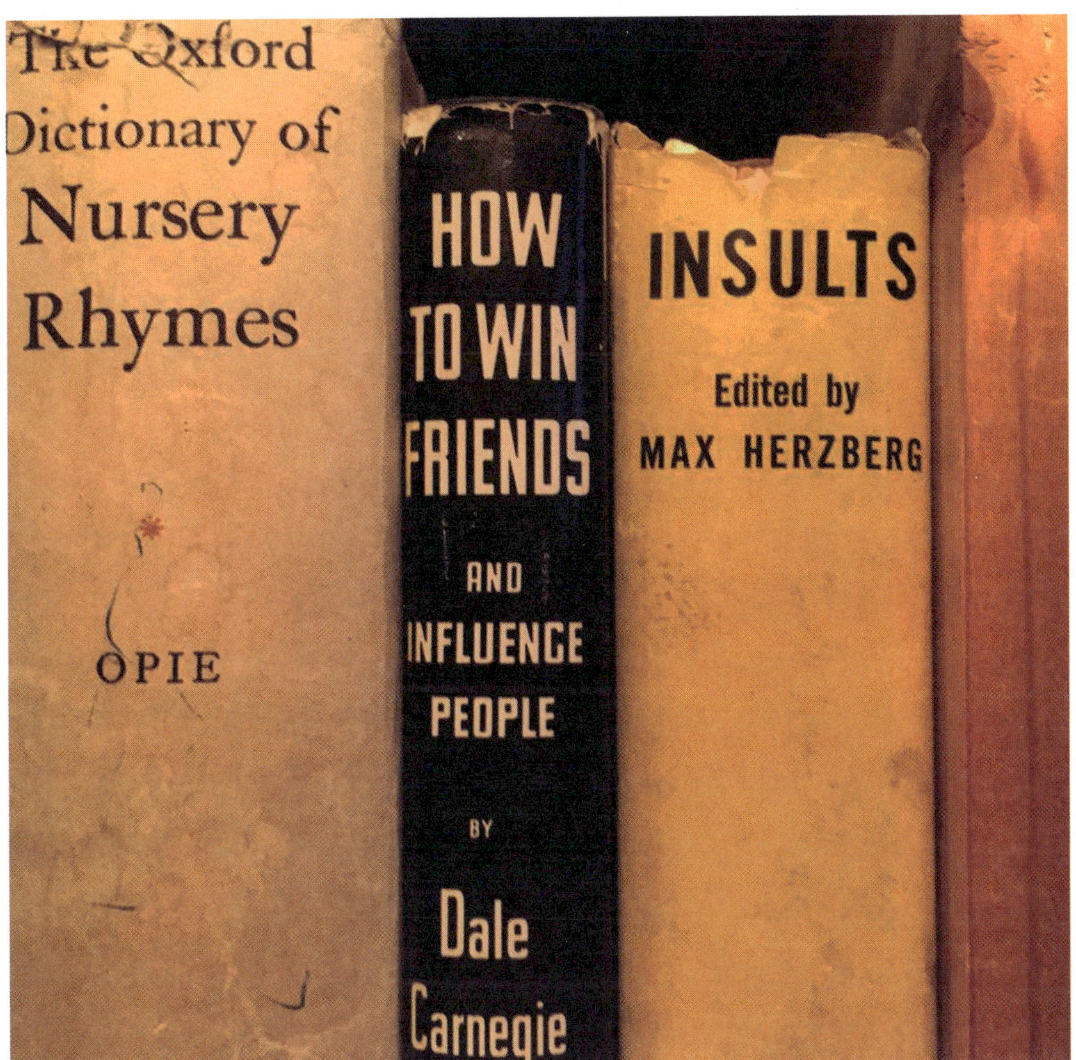

Books to have fun with.

HENRY JAMES: 'JANUARY 22'(1879). I heard some time ago, that Anthony Trollope had a theory that a boy might be brought up to be a novelist as to any other trade. He brought up – or attempted to bring up – his own son on this principle, and the young man became a sheep-farmer, in Australia.'

GARTH GREENWELL

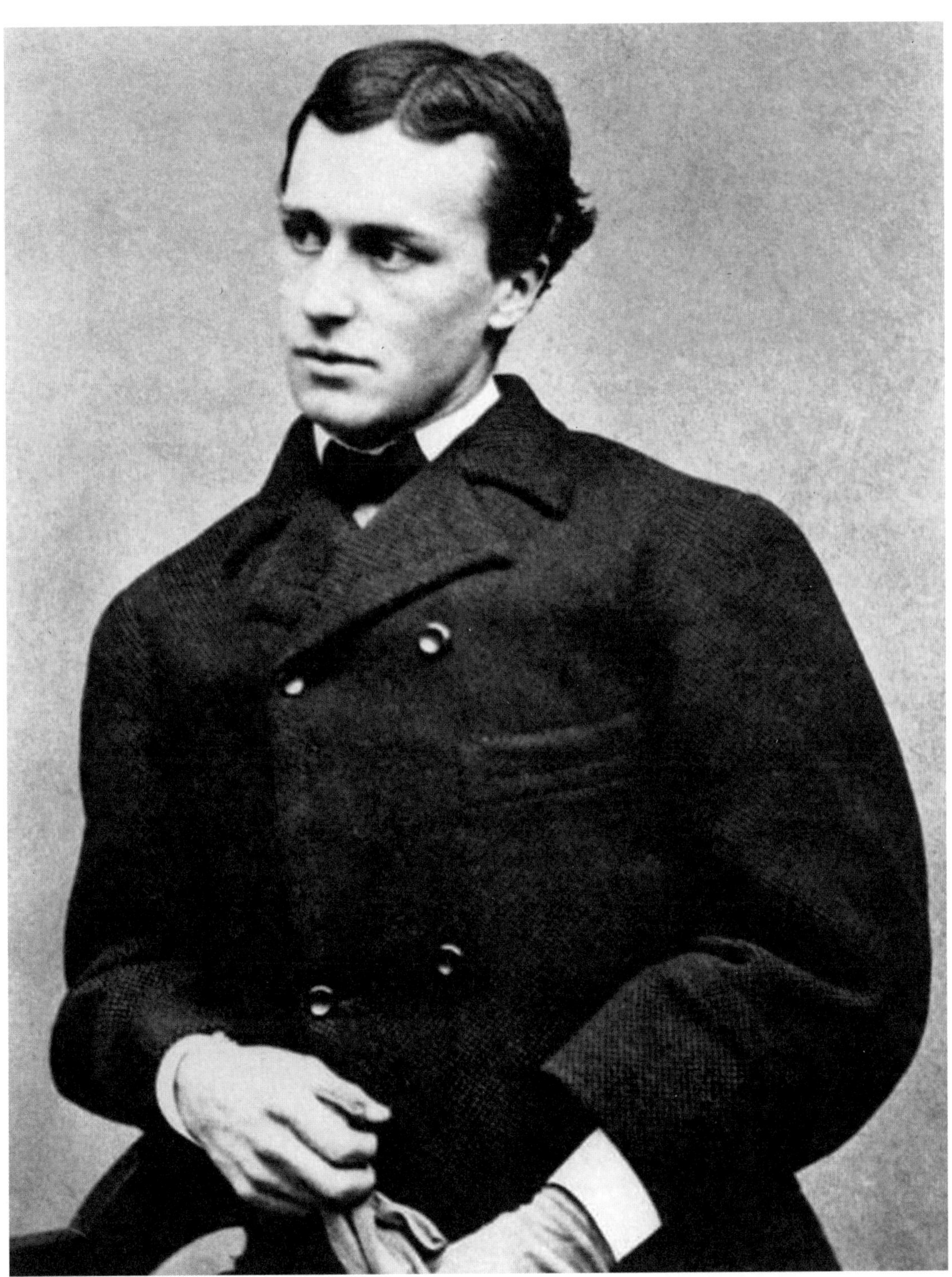

Happy Birthday, Henry James! I can't imagine my life without you.

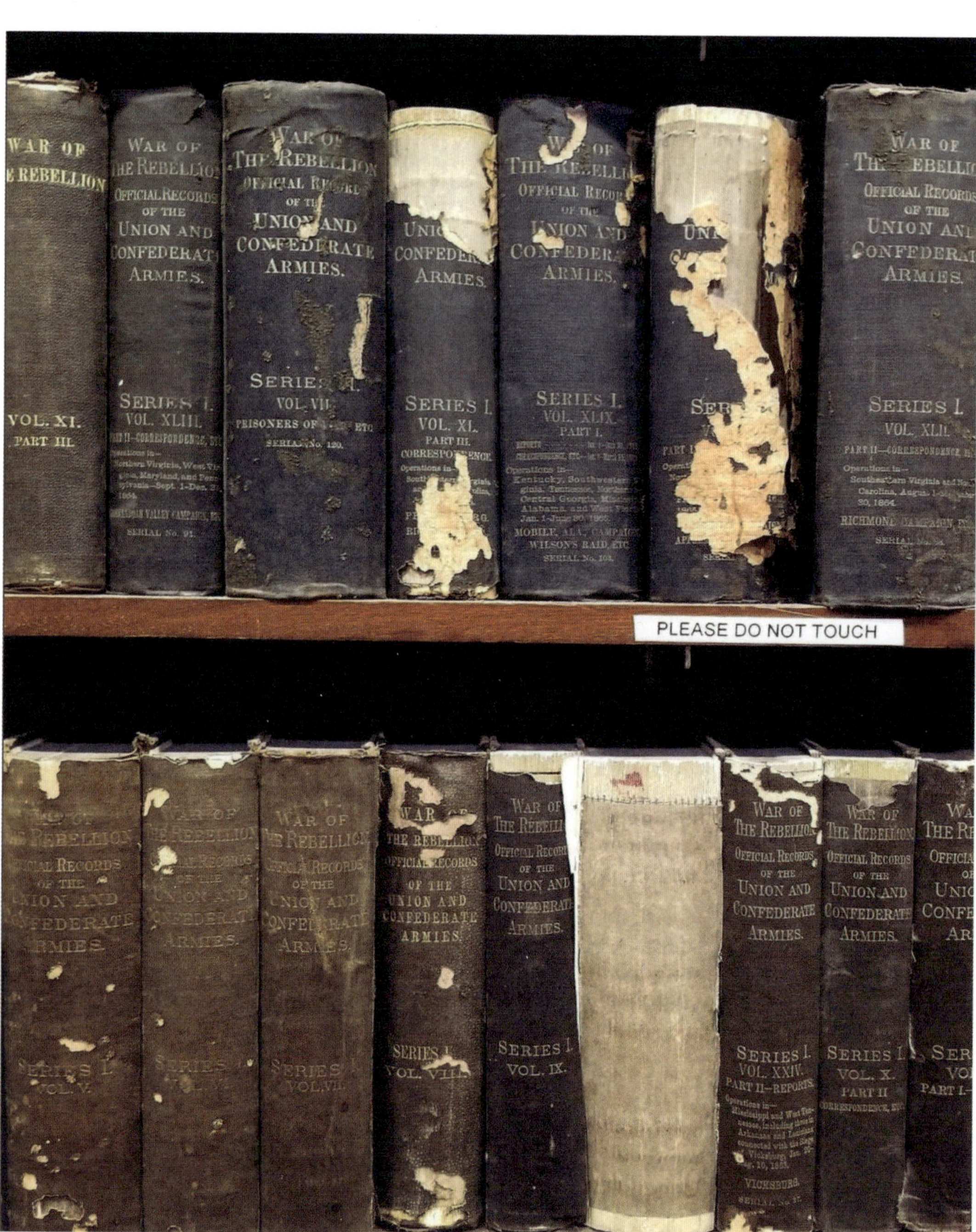

In the Waco Lodge Library, an edition of *The War of the Rebellion* (How the Civil War was referred to in the South). Travelling salesmen sold these to families who wanted to know where their family members ended up ... who was in what company and where that company fought.

2: where you are at

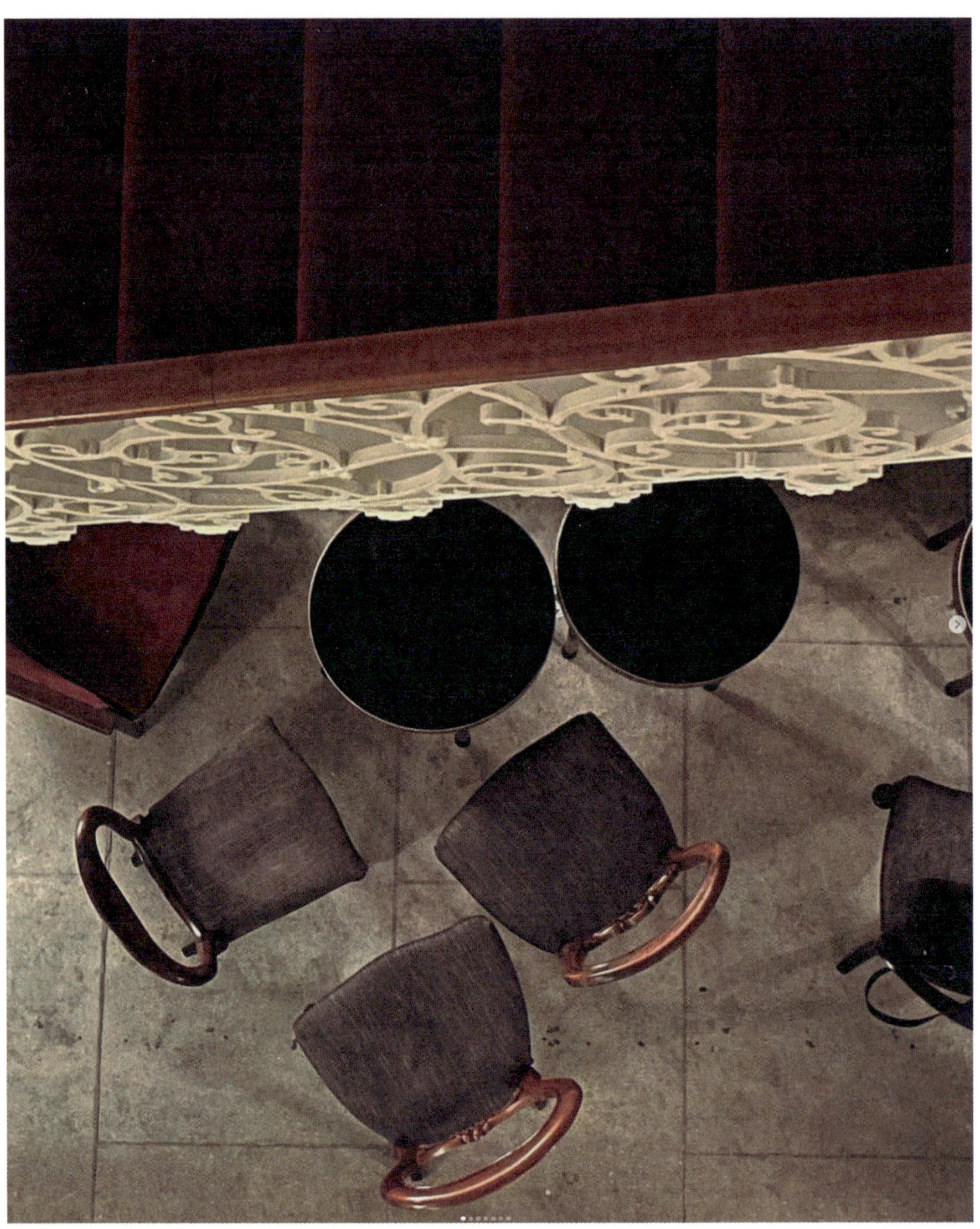

Agnisko Restaurant, London.

ANDREW JONES

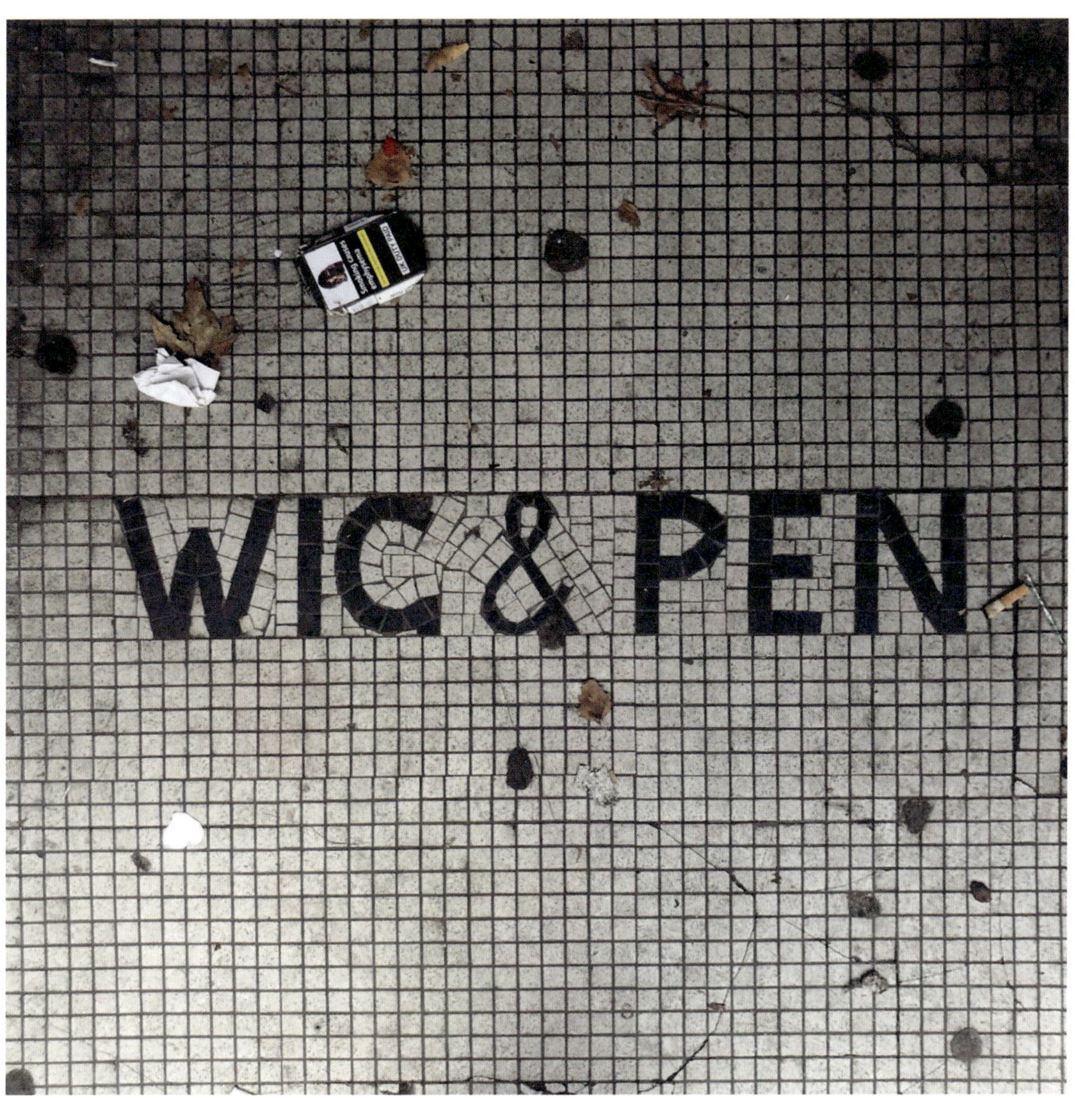

The old Wig & Pen Club, a club for lawyers and journalists which closed in 2003 after 95 years. Now standing empty having been occupied by a Thai restaurant chain. The building is said to be the only one to have survived the Fire of London of 1666.

CALUM STORRIE

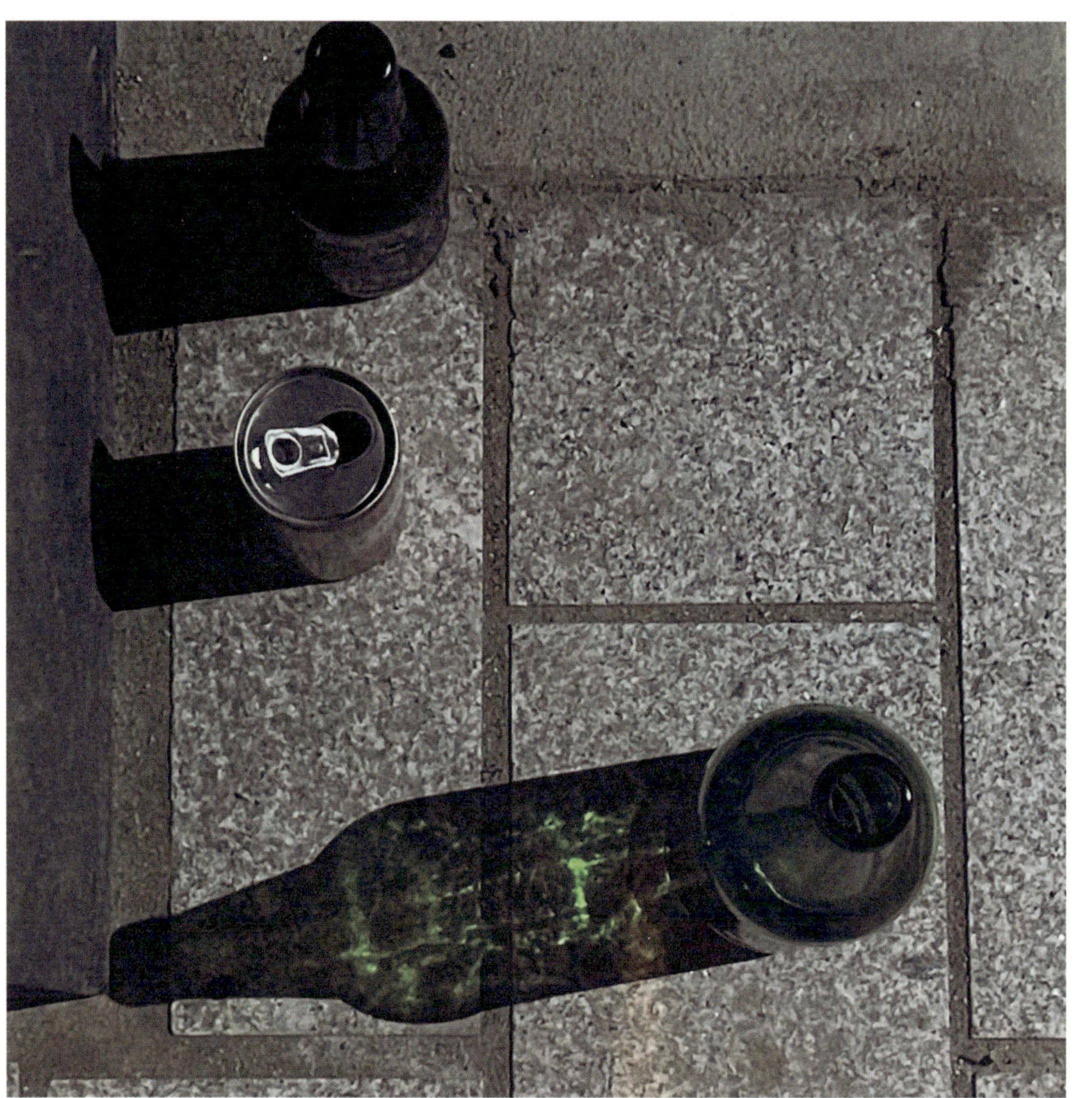

Somewhere in Hackney, late 1990s.

CORNELIA PARKER

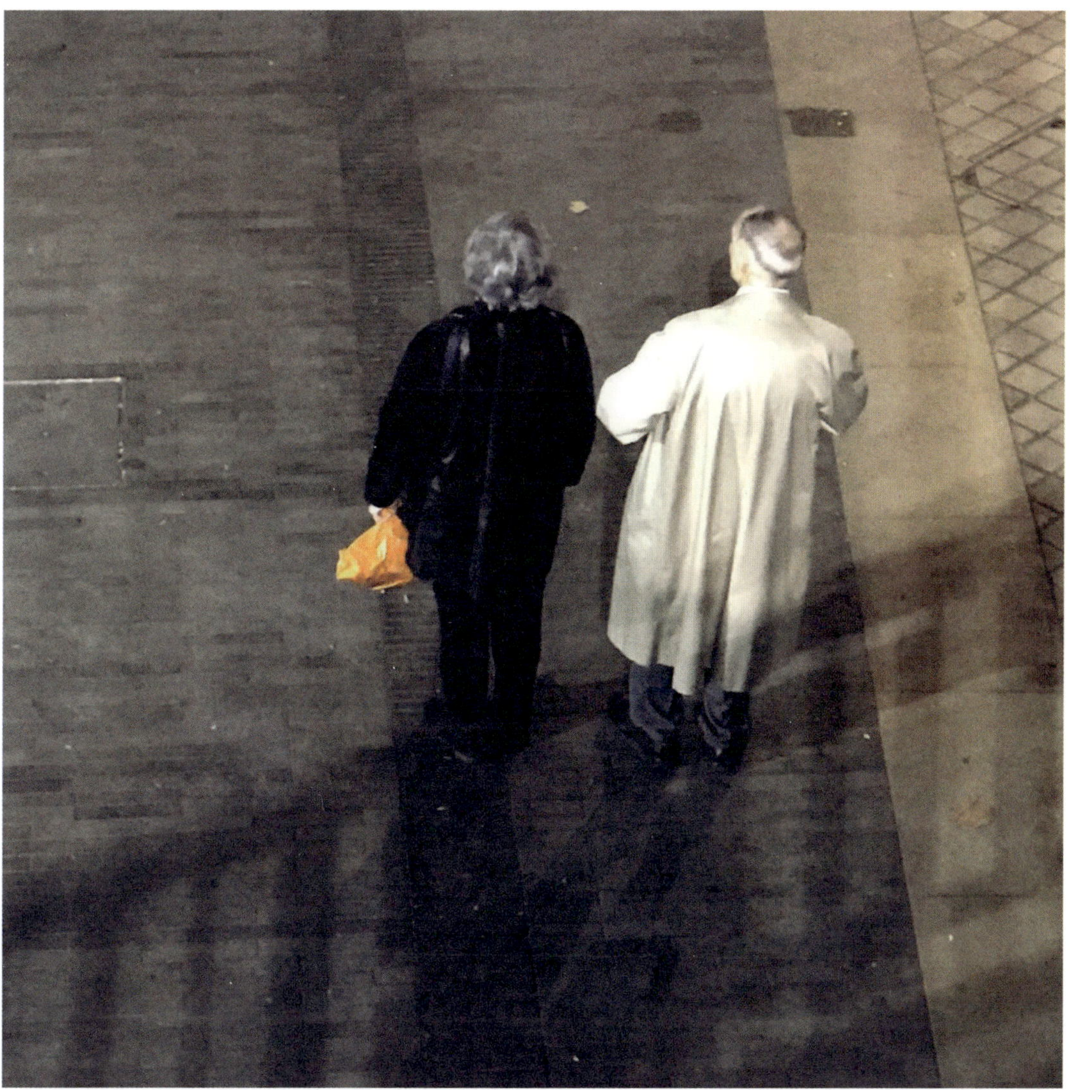

The couple.

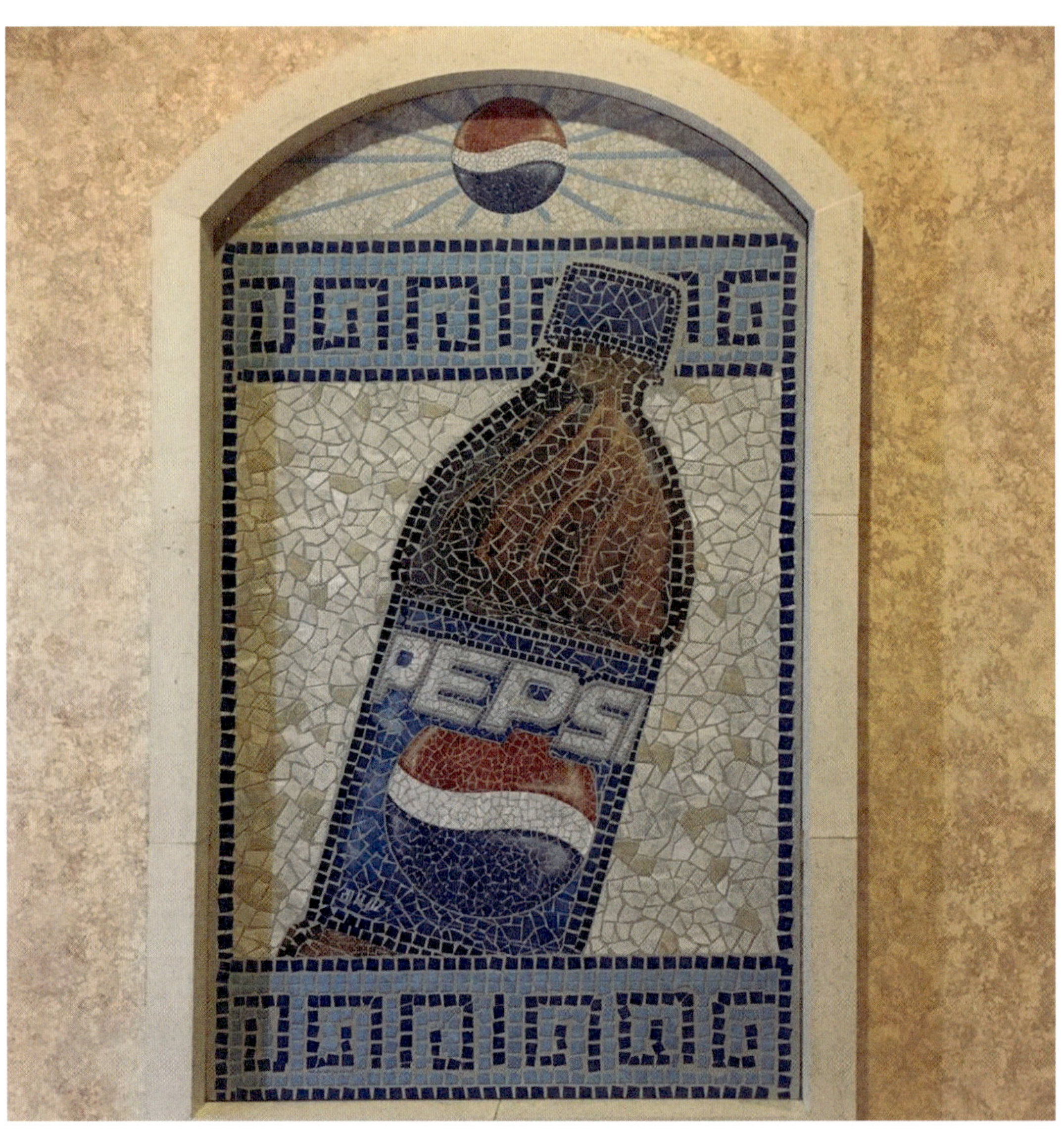

#lasvegas #thevenetian

CONRAD SHAWCROSS

Courtesy of the Artist

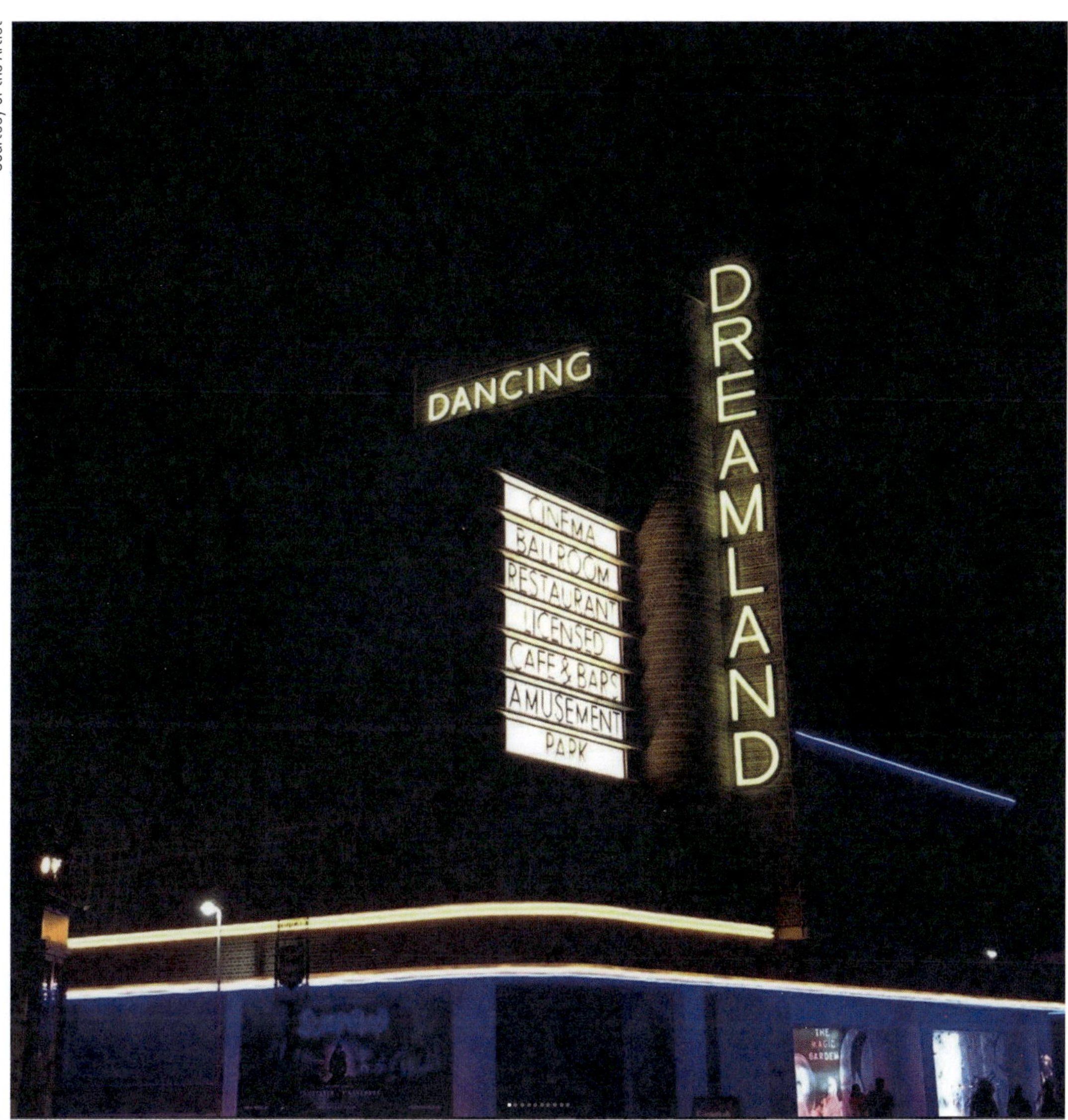

#Margate.

TRAVELLING INTO AND OUT OF CITIES by rail, I see houses not as they pose for the streets but before they've shaved or put on their make-up: tatty back gardens, rusting fire escapes, rain-puddled trampolines in muddy gardens, improvised party spaces on the roofs of cowboy extensions, compost, mulch, everything unkempt. A woman leans far out, smoking, from a window in a flat in which she's not allowed to smoke. A man steps out of the shower. How many books are being written, one keystroke after another, in back rooms and bad light, that I'll never know about? It's all evidence of something, and observing it feels like an invasion of privacy.

ASSEMBLED AT THE MEETING POINT, newly arrived foreign students will be given maps, directions, timetables, contact numbers. Most will stick to the schedule; one or two will stray, go walkabout, become lost – which is the best thing they can do, being the whole point of travel. (In stories, when someone gets lost you know something interesting or even magical is going to happen.) Getting lost at home, in a district choked with habit and familiarity, is harder (this is where drugs come in), but happily there are still times when I feel I hardly know this place, I've only a slim idea of where I am.

COLIN ROBINSON

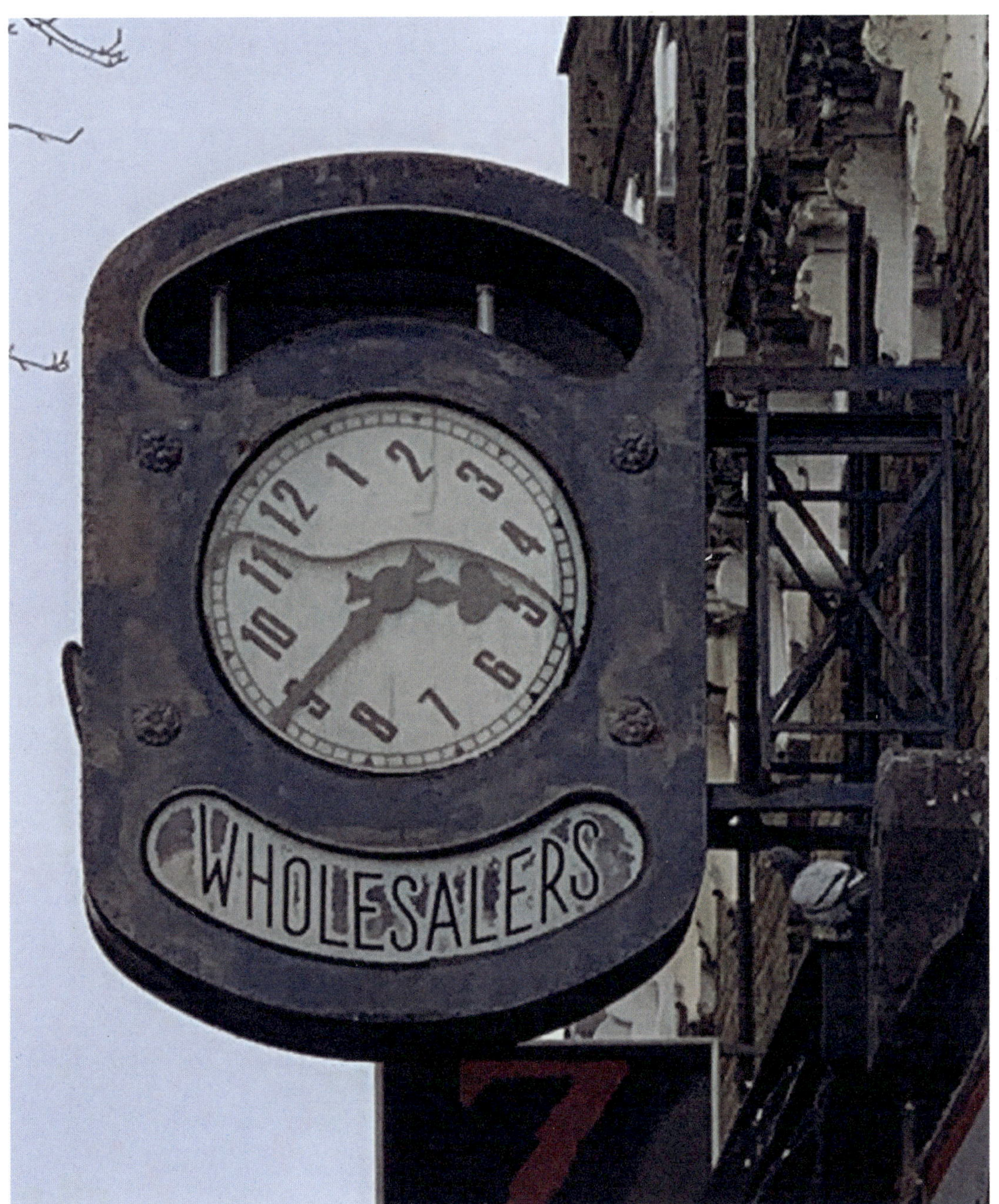

Time askew in Stoke Newington, North London.

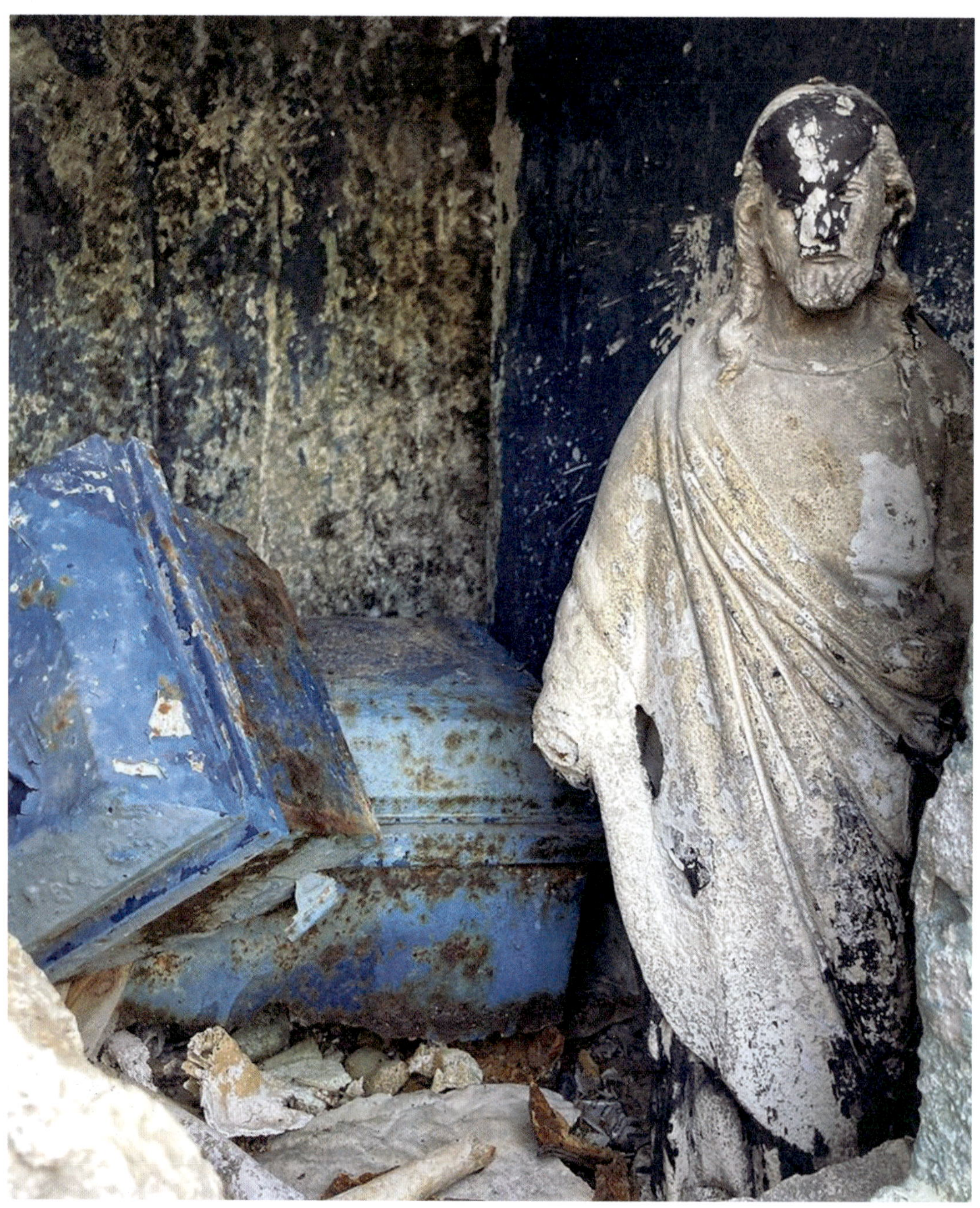

Cemetario General, Mexico.

MARK SALVATUS

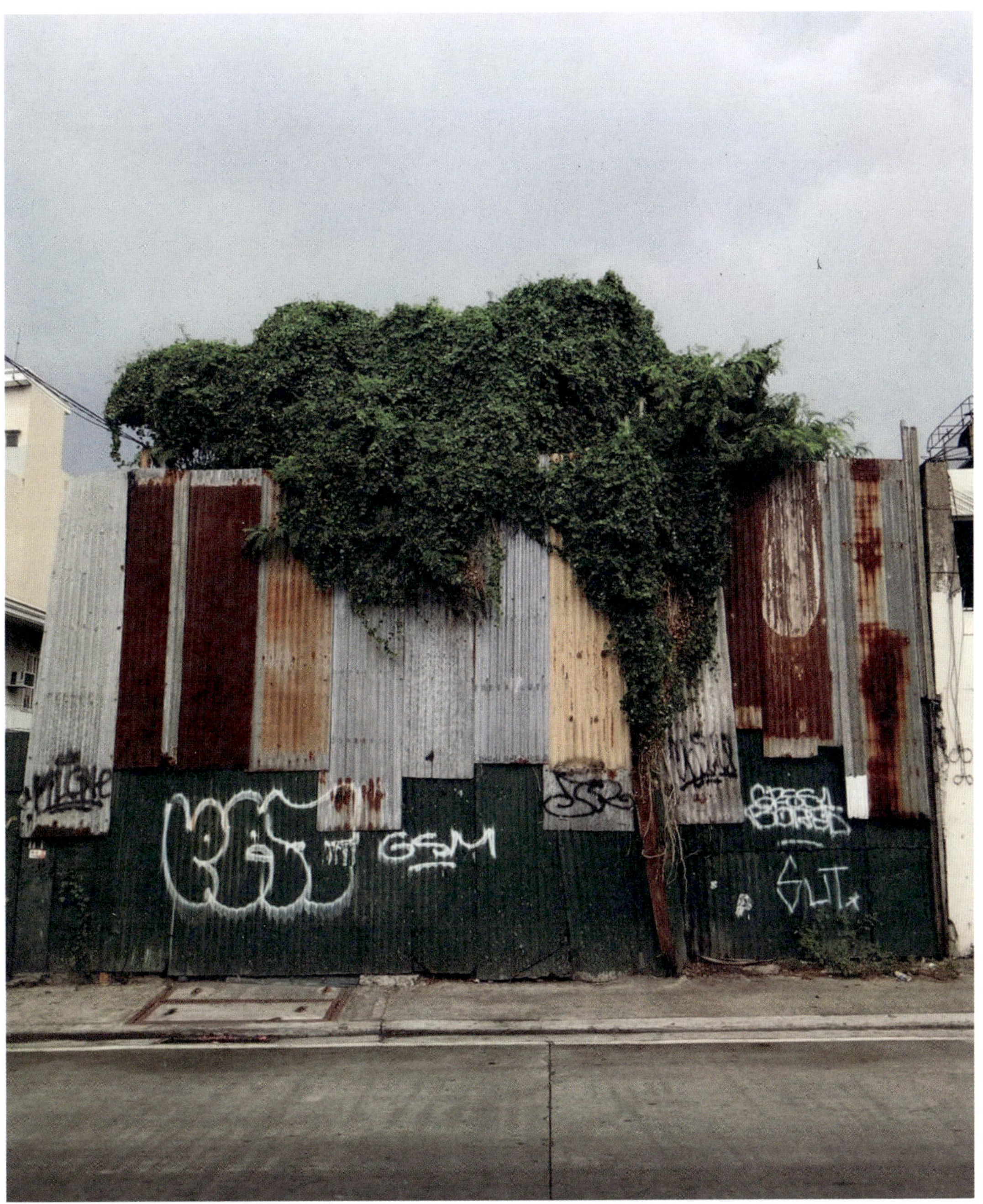

Cubao, Quezon City, Philippines.

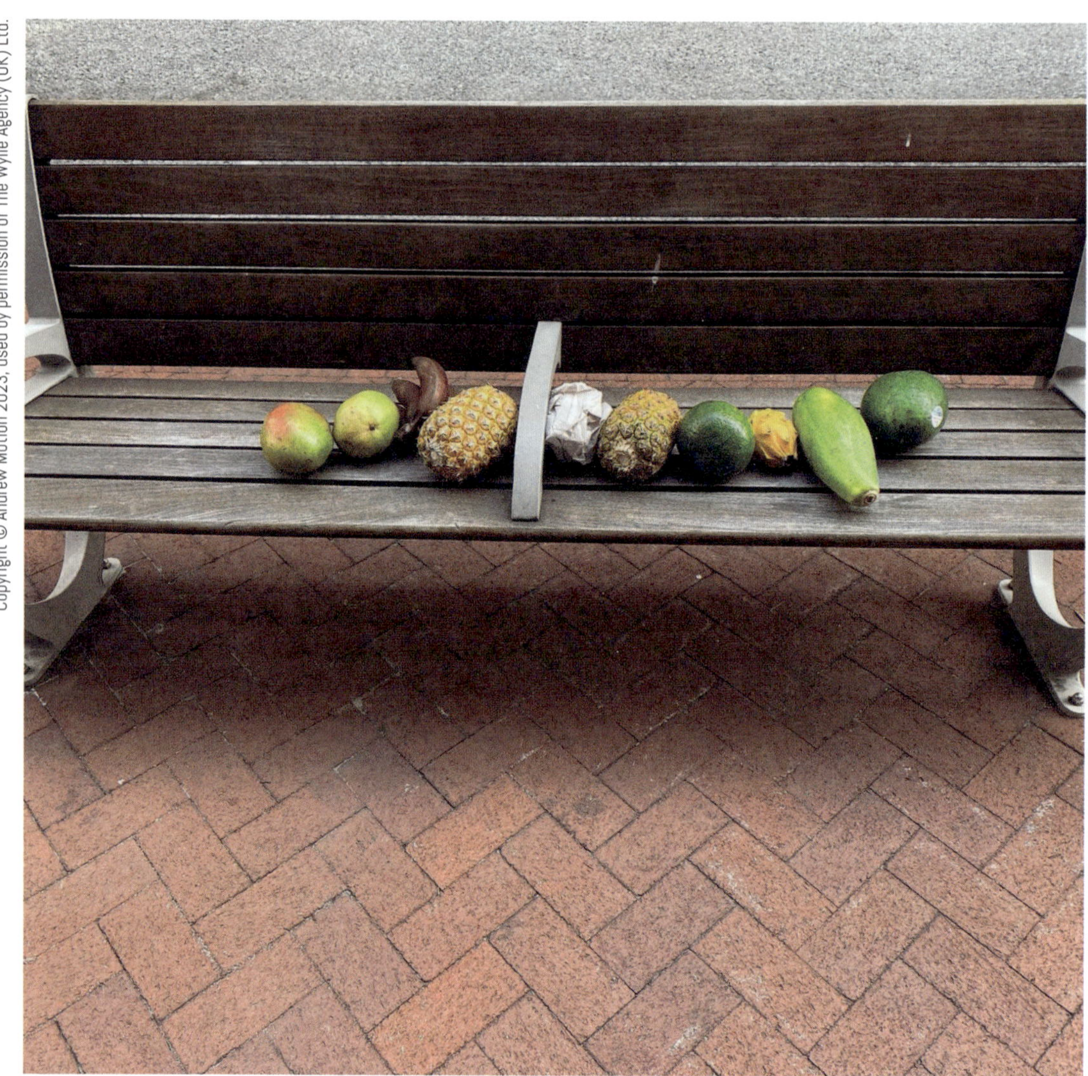

Tired fruit.

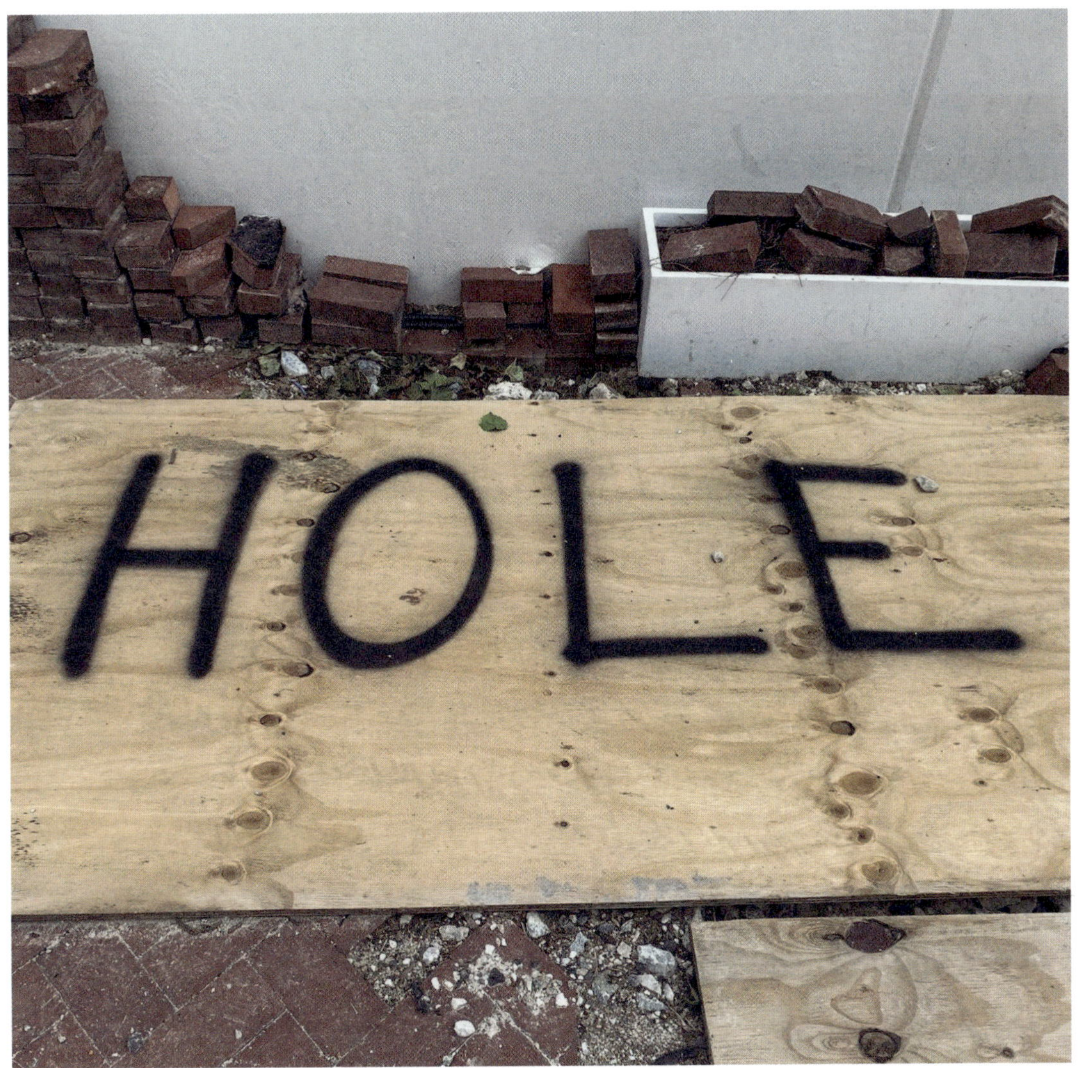

Baltimore. Where they tell it like it is.

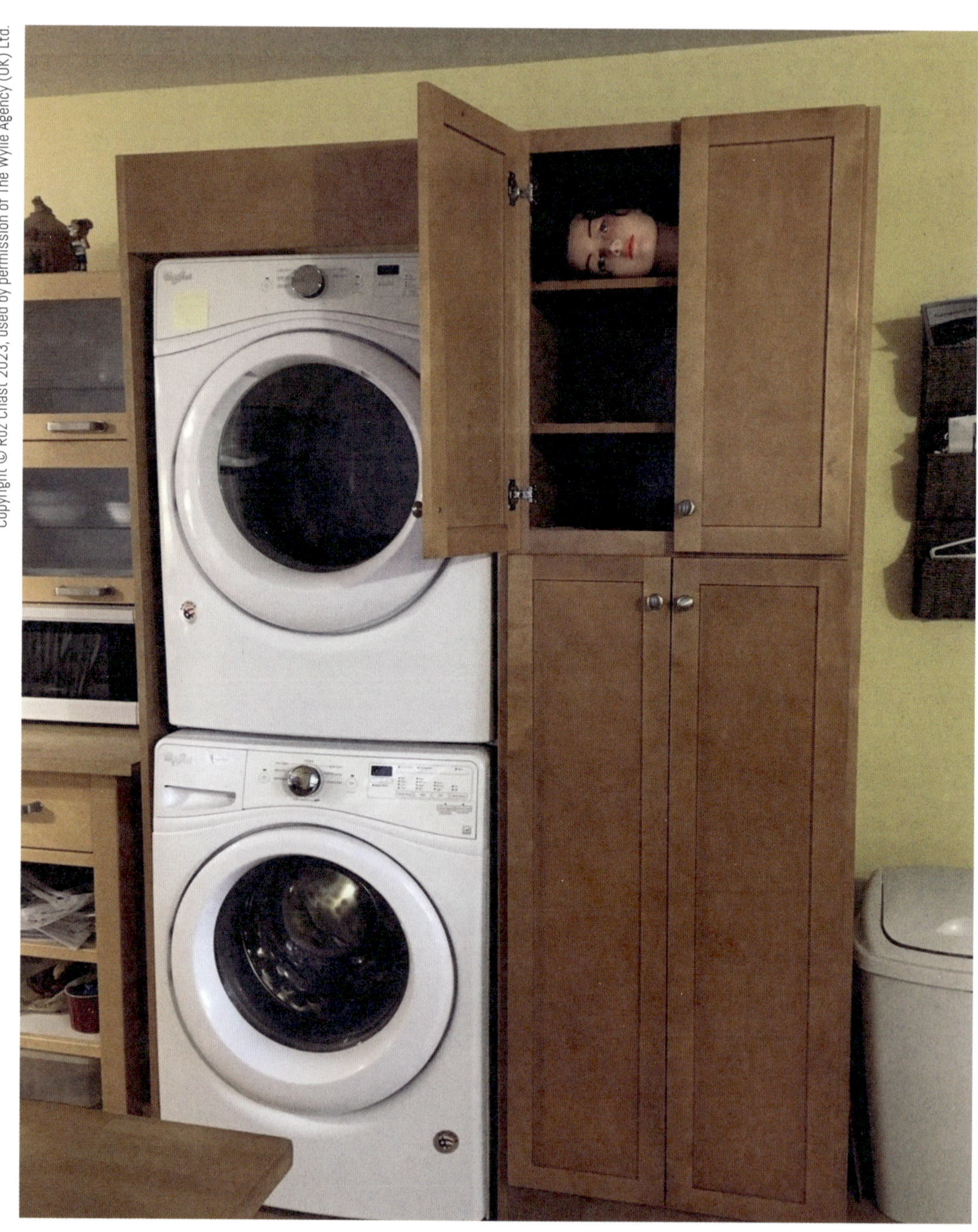

The house we're renting on vacation has a washer dryer and some other things.

ROZ CHAST

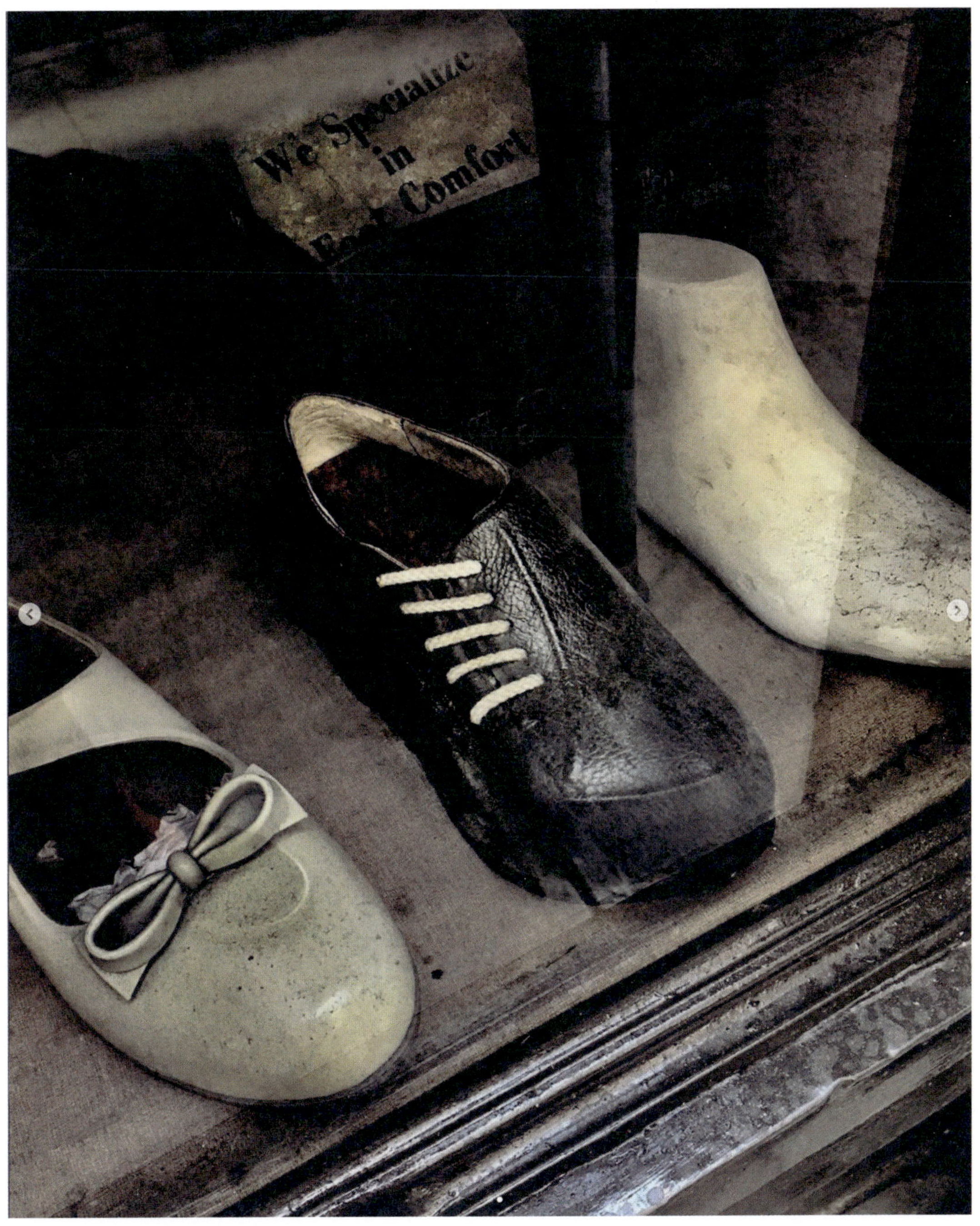

A shoe store in midtown from The Past ... close-up of window. My mother wore shoes like the one in the middle. They were called 'Murray Space Shoes'.

Tonight: male hydrant with
female shadow

ROZ CHAST

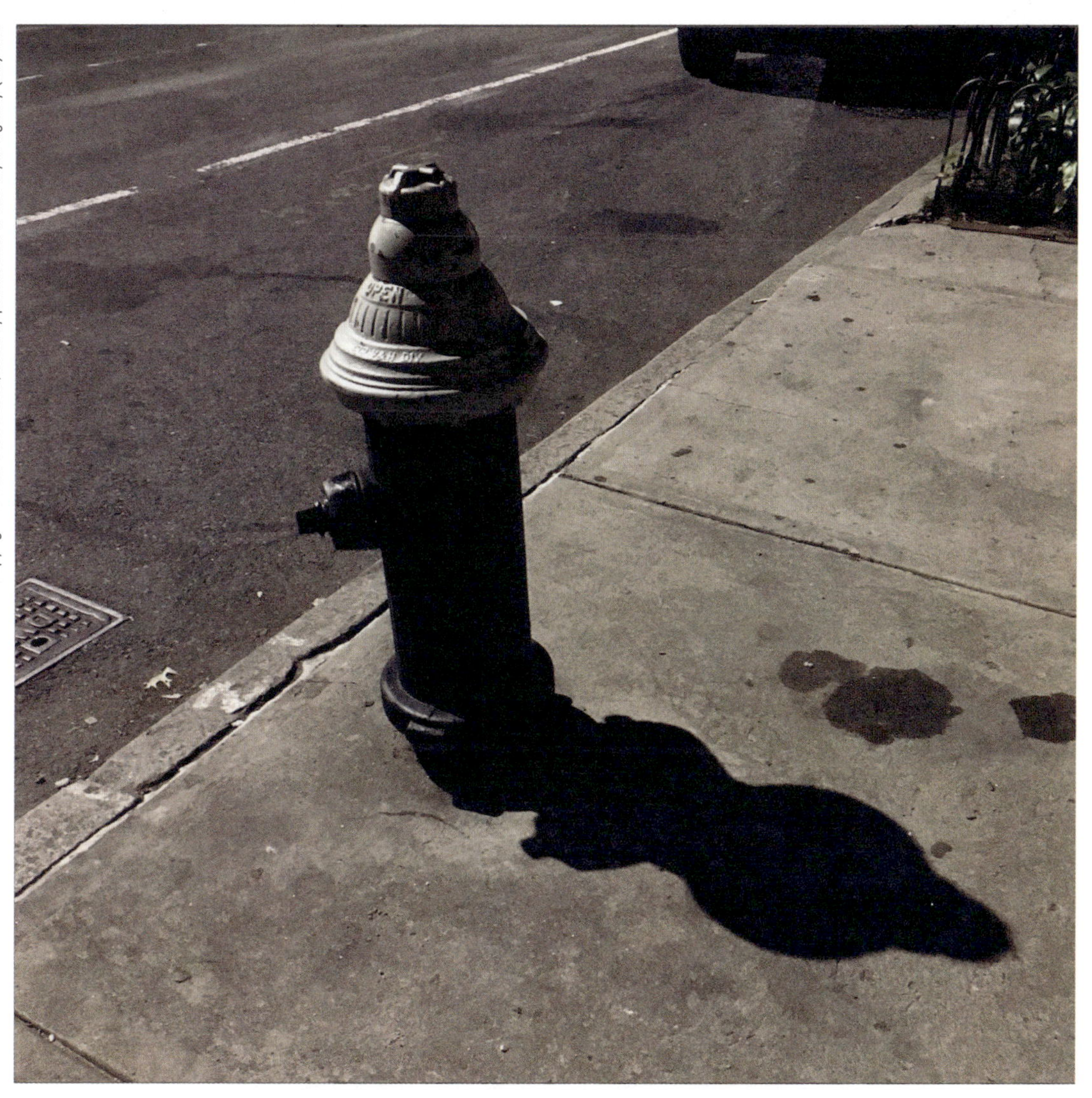

ROZ CHAST

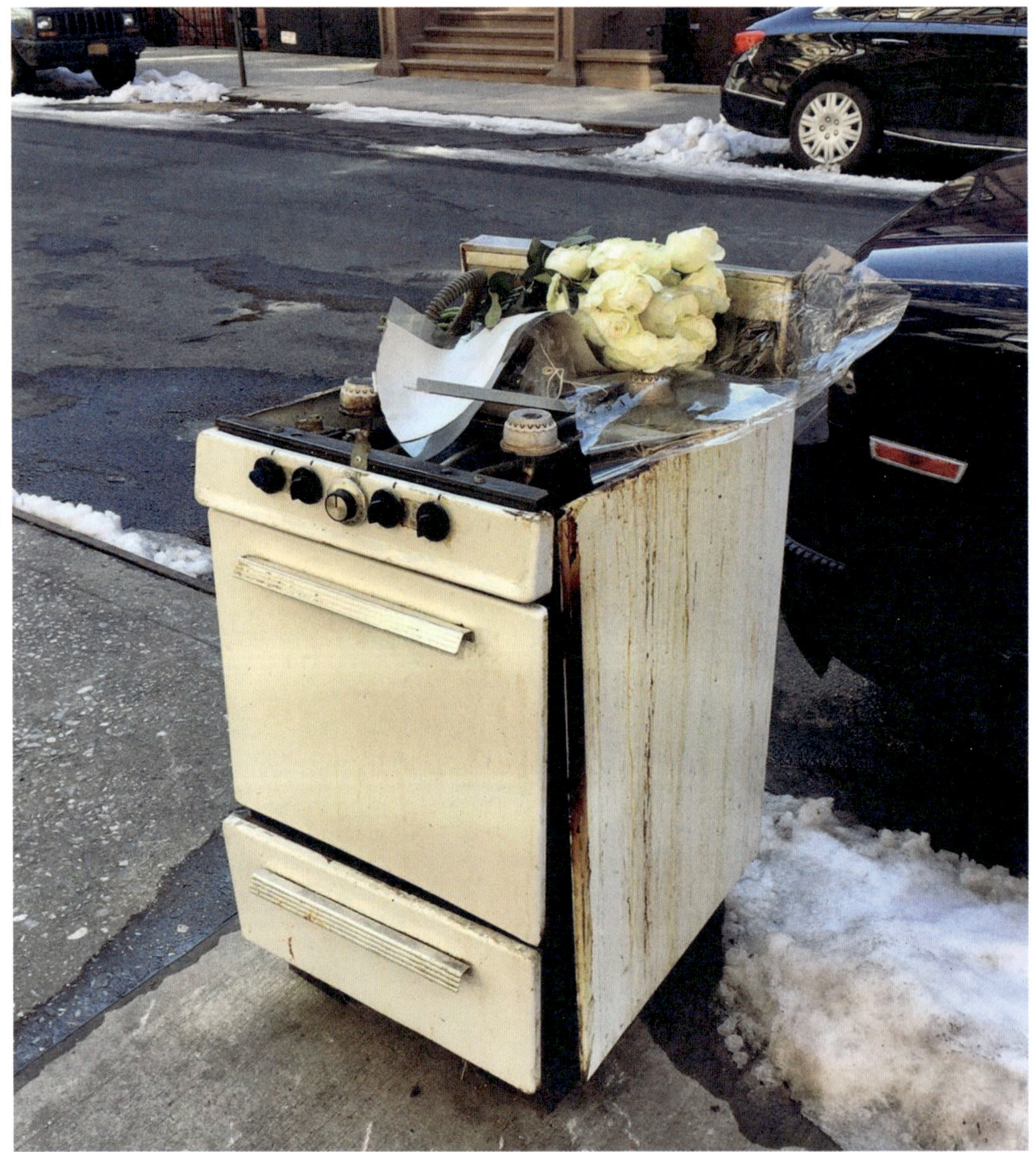

Fuck you and your dozen roses.

Also I'm not cooking anymore.

Happy Valentine's Day.

MID-AFTERNOON ON A WEEKDAY in March 2023 in the City of London: half an hour after a thunderous shower of rain the sky turns unaccountably pink, as if a wind has blown north from a red desert, carrying sand of such fine grain it is barely material, and with the light a silence. Something is happening that nobody knows how to speak about, something awful but also releasing, but into what? The markets get the jitters.

Traffic slows, as around the scene of an accident. On the pavements, pedestrians step carefully around pink puddles.

Someone is reminded of something but cannot remember what (something biblical, something in a dream?). Someone confesses to their partner that they have been leading a double life for years and the partner says, *You think I don't know?* Someone runs a hot bath. Someone pours a triple whisky. Someone sings a song they didn't even know they knew the words to. Someone tells another someone they love them and someone else makes rapid use of the office shredding machine. Someone goes out to buy a sandwich and is never seen again. Someone sees God. Someone unlocks a drawer and stares dully at what is inside. Someone phones their mother for the first time in twenty years and someone else throws a brick through a shop window. Someone carries on working, head down. Someone takes a sleeping pill, and a few more to make sure. Someone laughs, someone cries.

The pinkness in the air fades, dissolves or becomes transparent. A meteorologist with sideburns is interviewed on the 10-o'clock news and the markets pick up. The puddles evaporate.

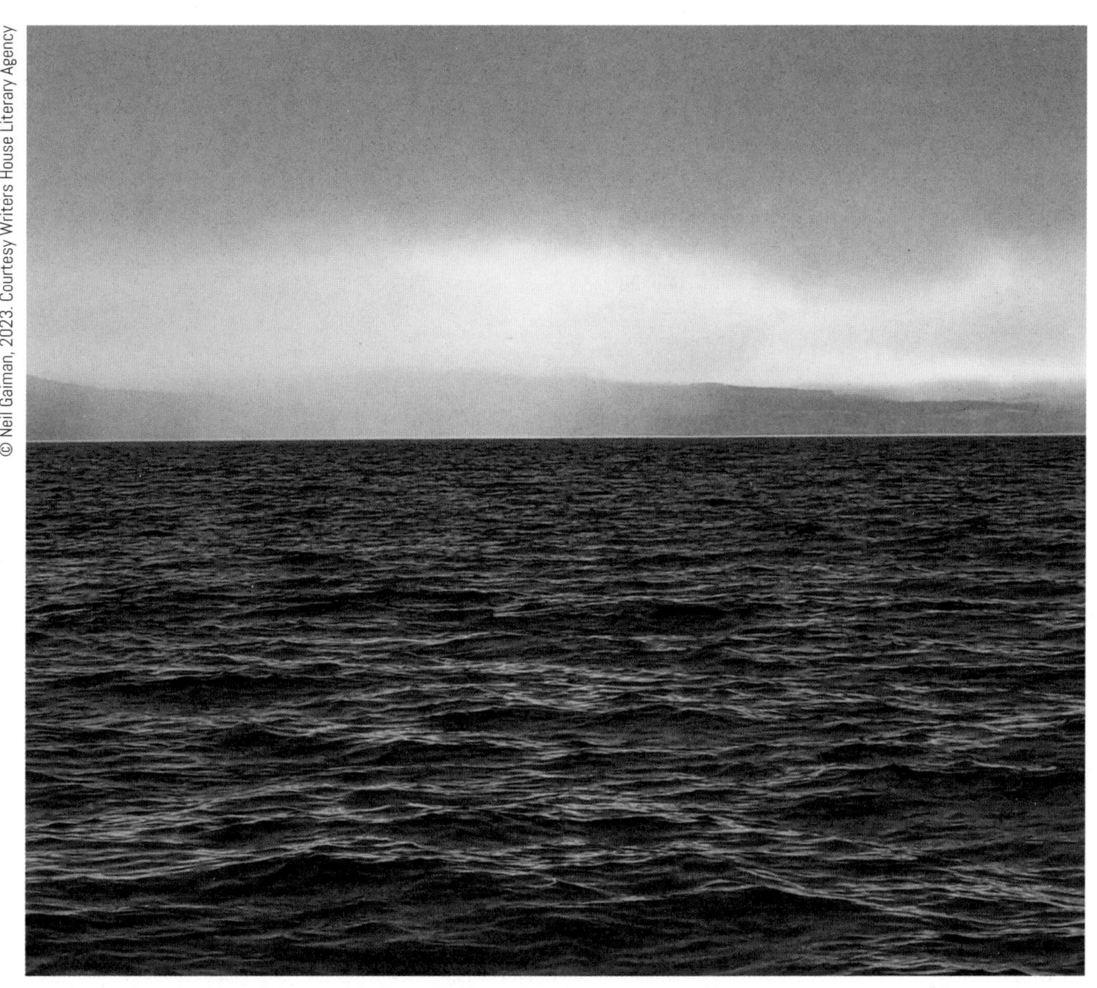

A colour photo. No filters. This is what the world actually looked like this morning, in the mist and the rain.

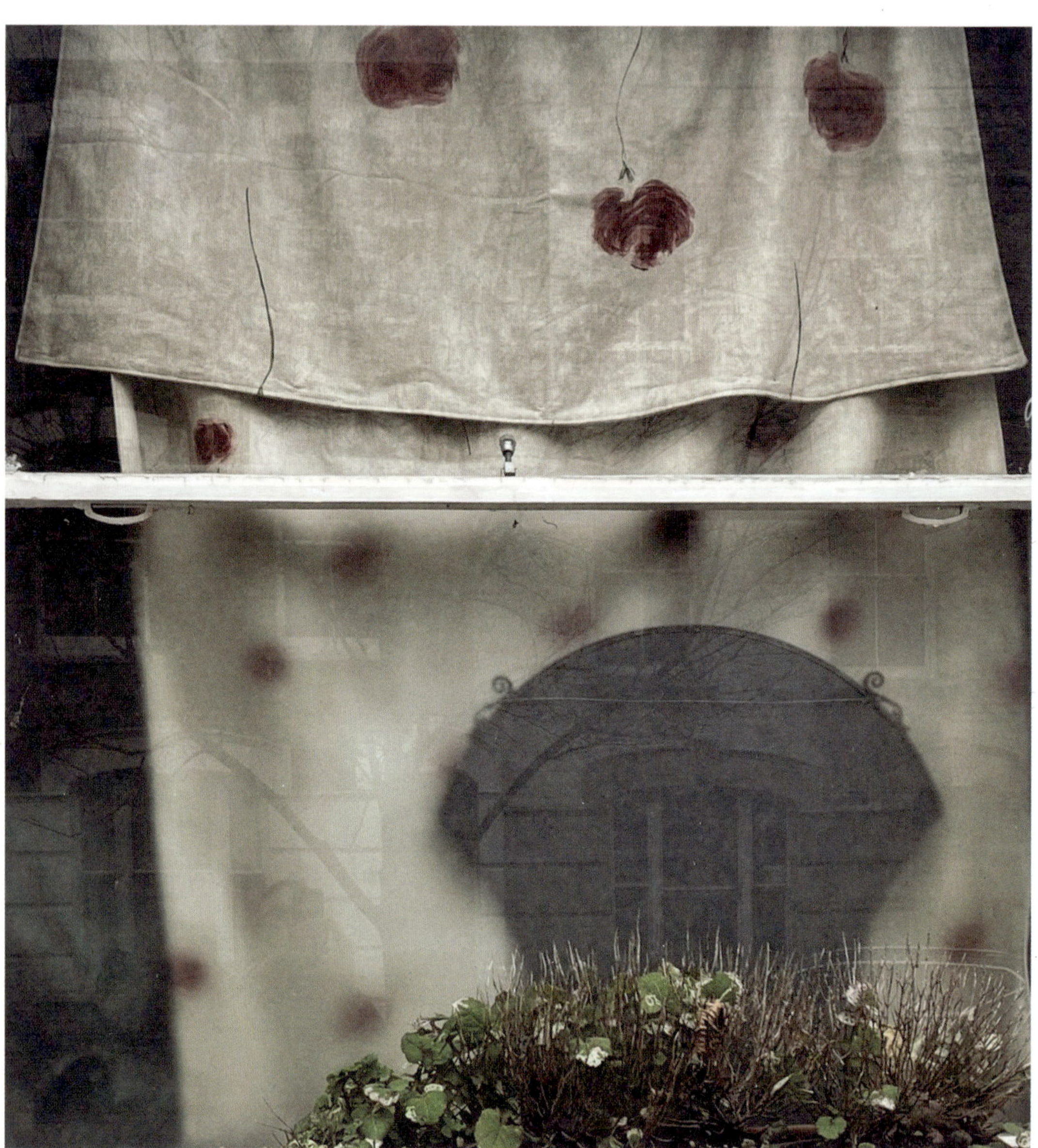

Windows.

CORNELIA PARKER

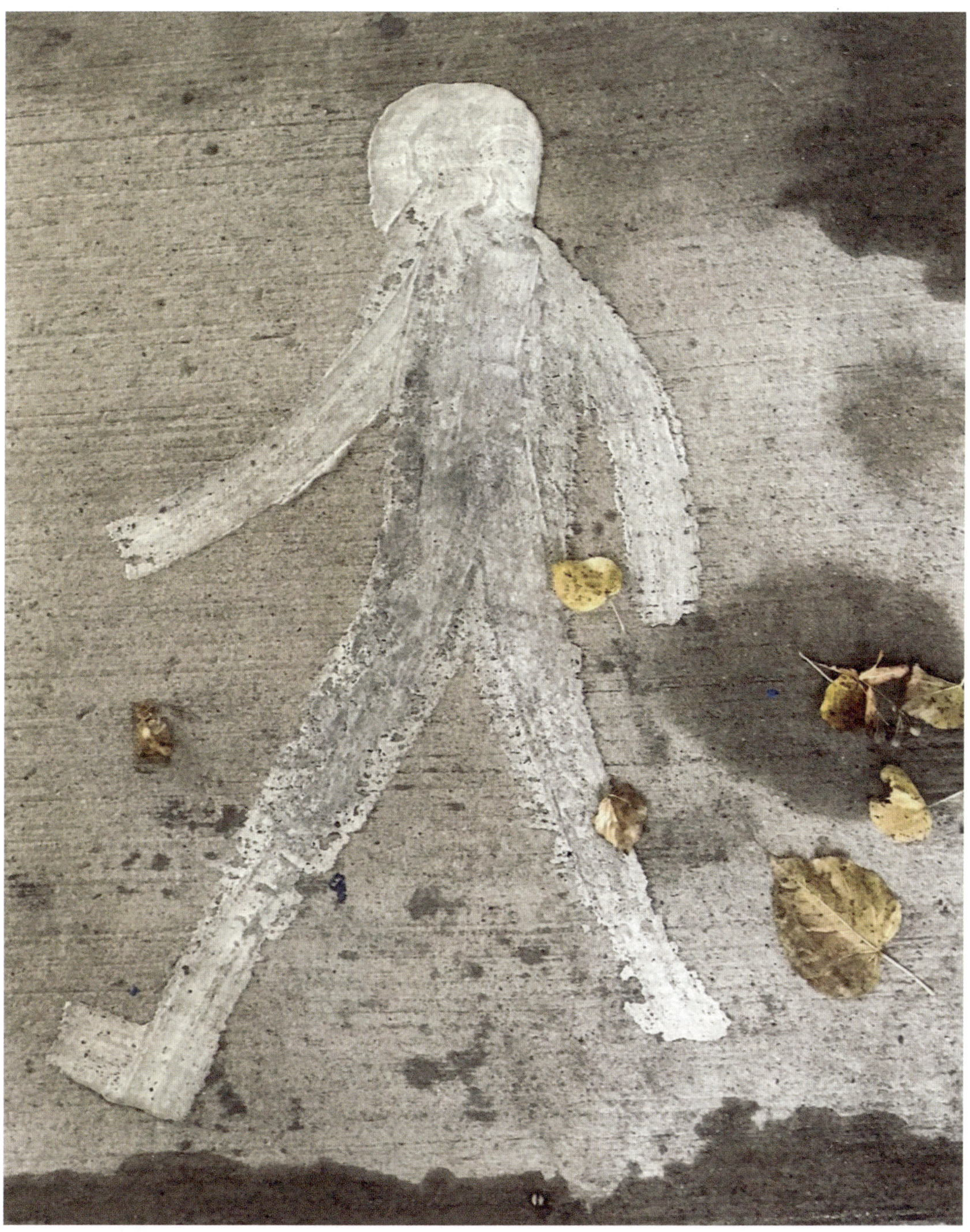

Weather's changing.

BOBBIE OLIVER

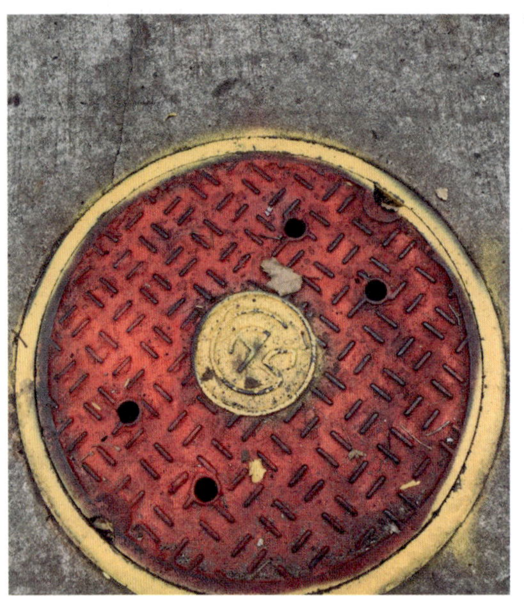

Ancient Indian mandala found on Brooklyn street.

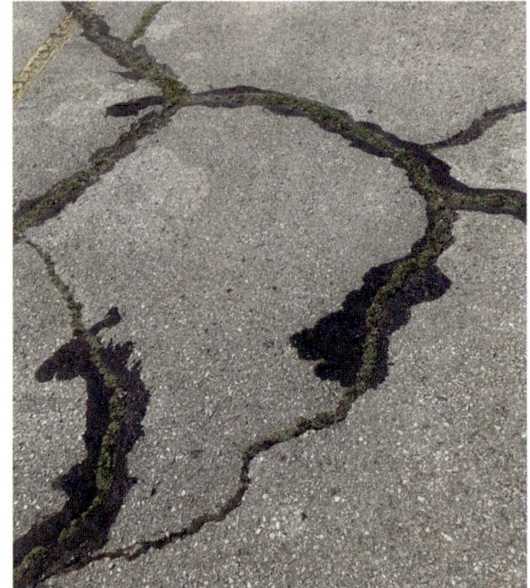

Cracks.

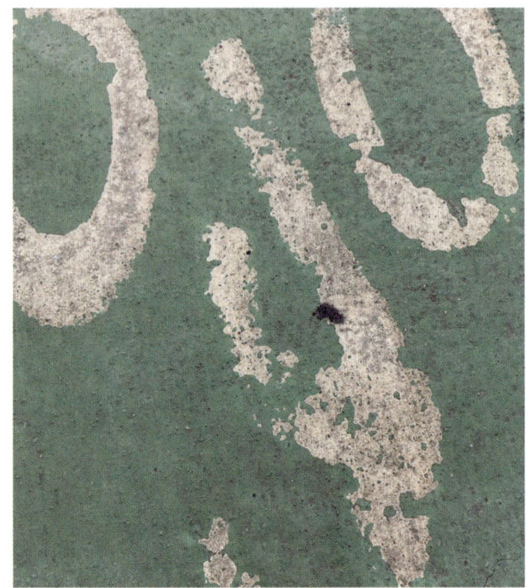

Street Painting.

CORNELIA PARKER

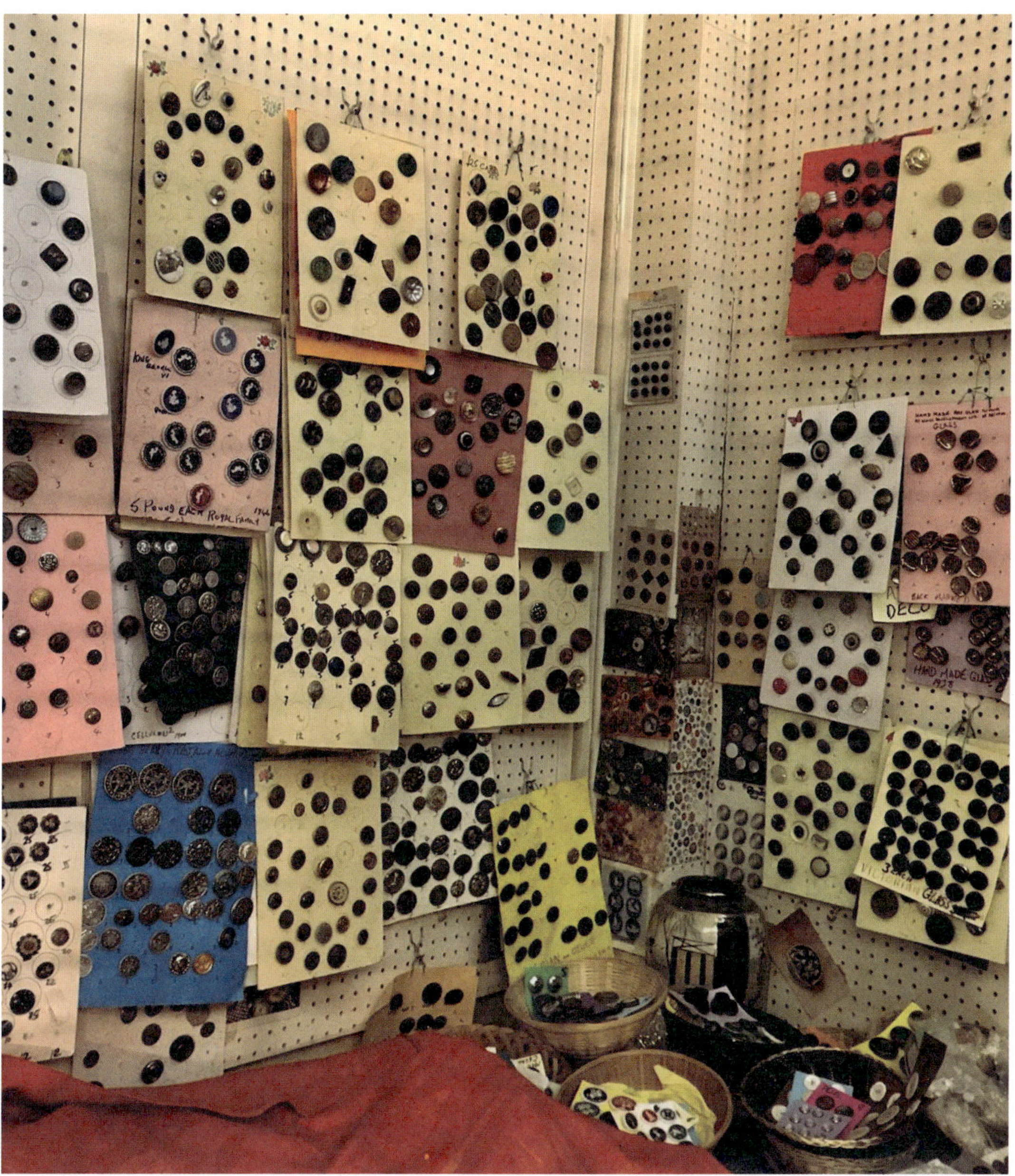

Buttons.

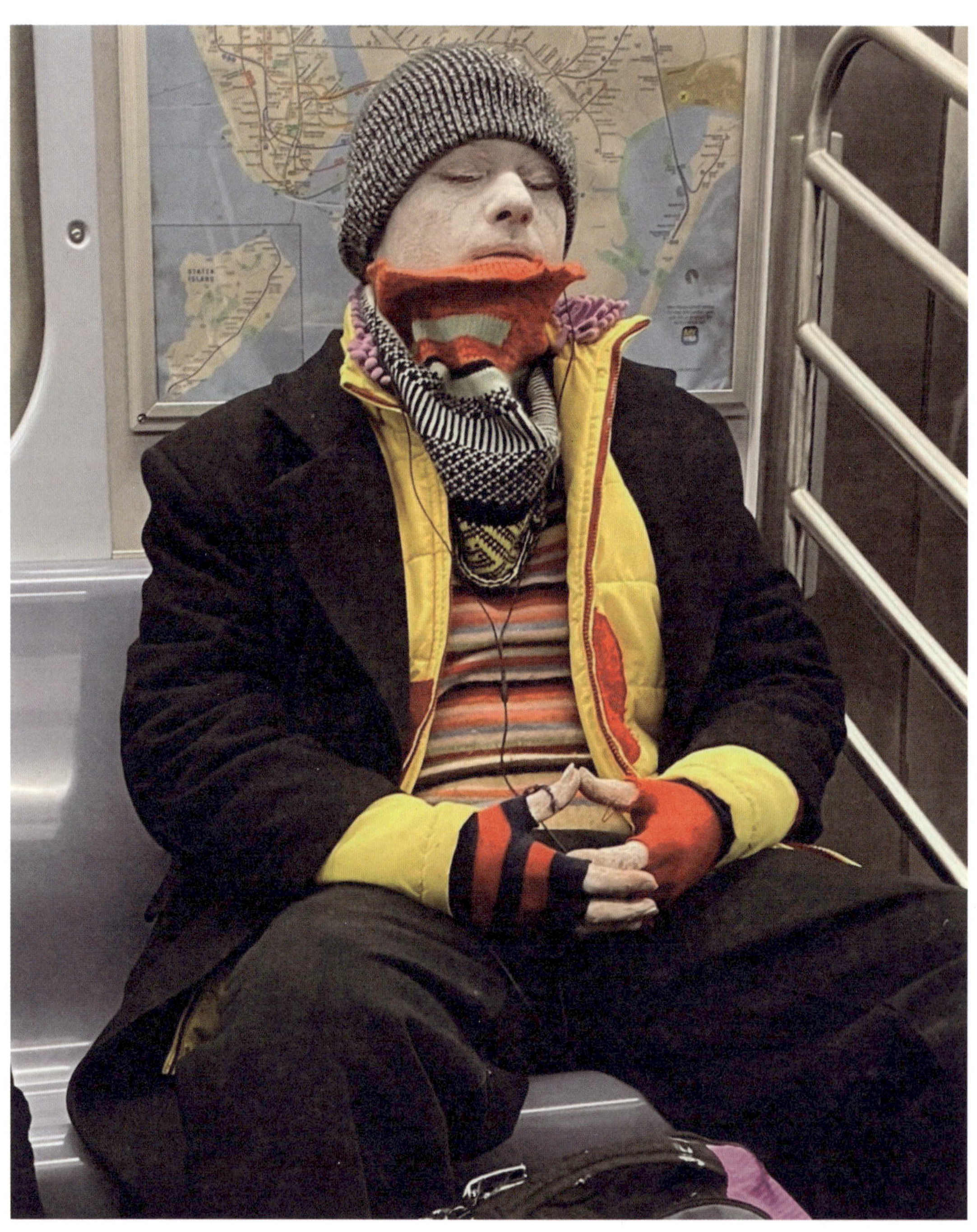

Even clowns have to commute.

BOBBIE OLIVER

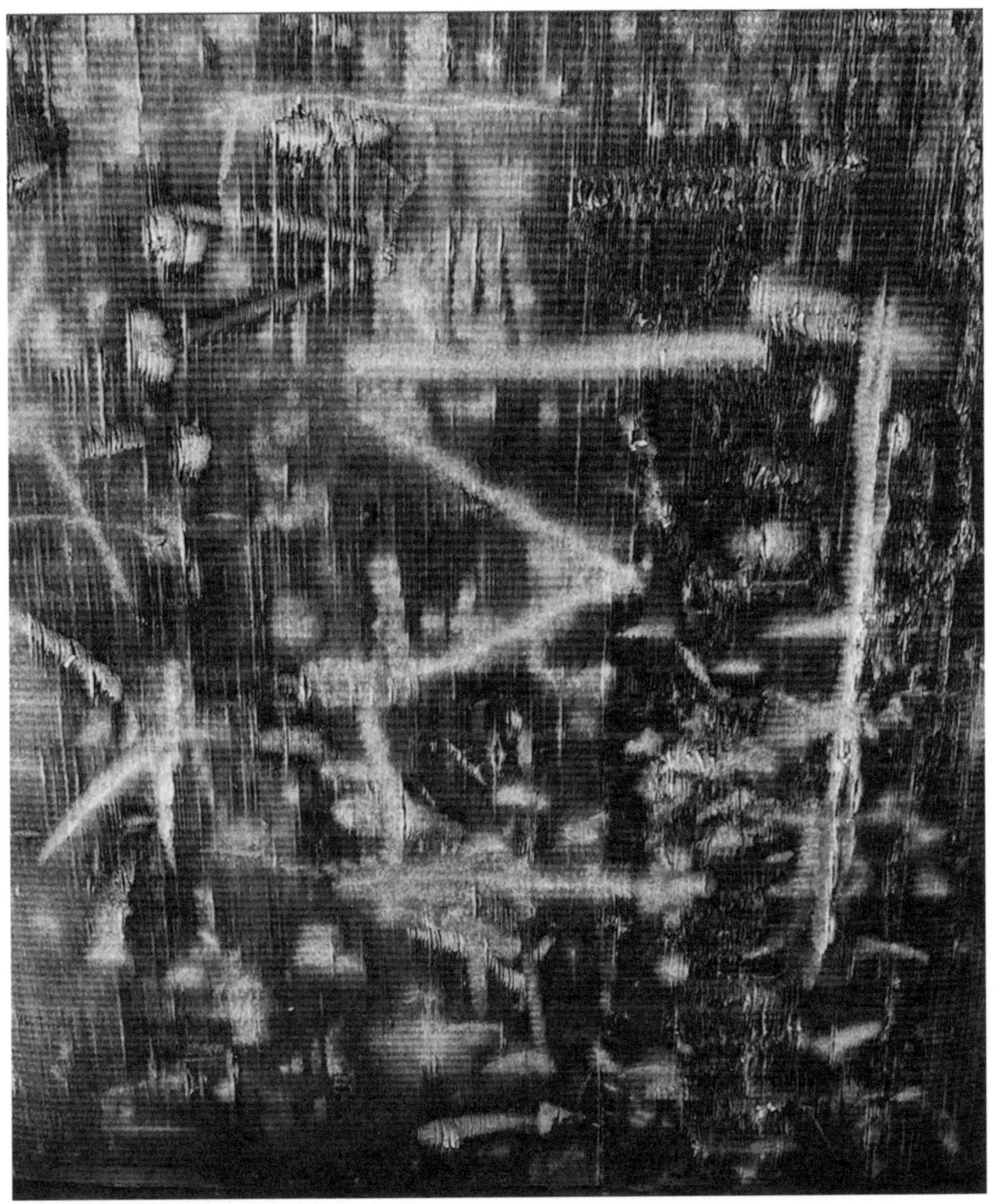

NYC air-conditioner screen.

VARIOUS

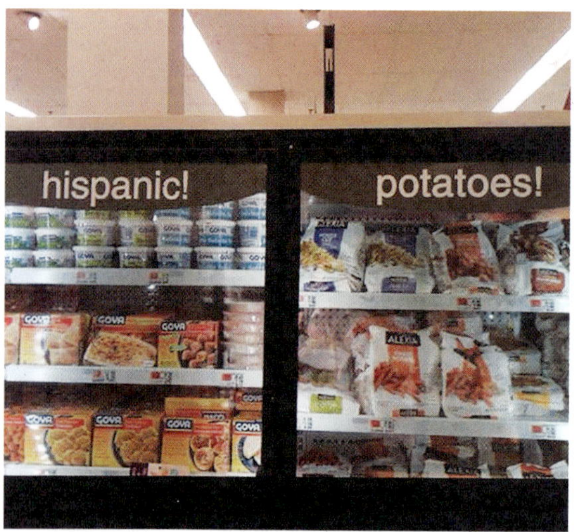

Lucien Kee.

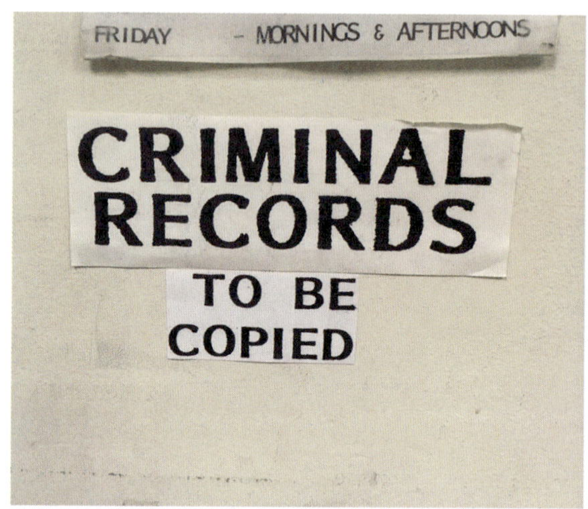

Carey Young.

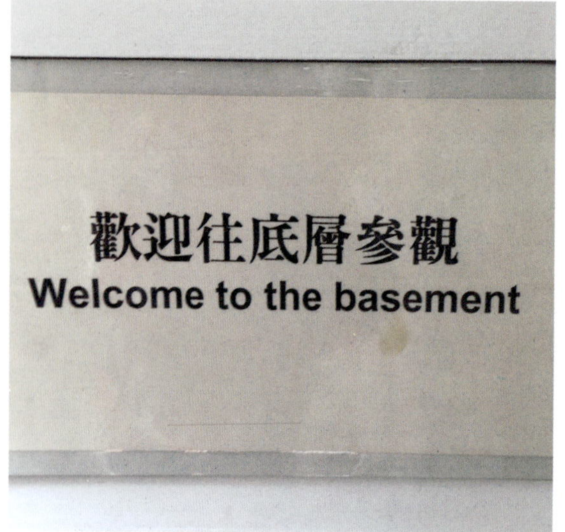

Kamila Shamsie.

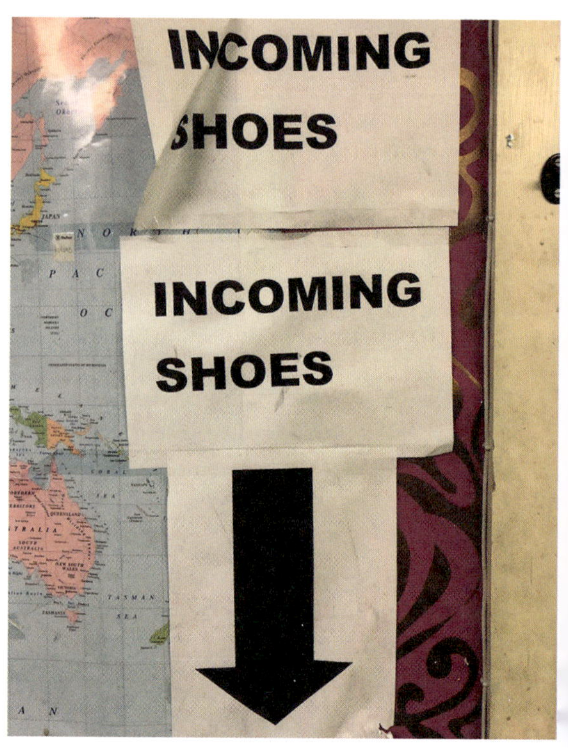

Calum Storrie.

I USED TO THINK signs like NO BALL GAMES were clues (some of them anagrams: MANGO LABELS) in a kind of treasure hunt, and that if I solved them all, and in the right order, then I'd win a prize. Now I realise that they are put in place by a hidden brotherhood of priests desperate to resist a rising tide of blasphemy and impurity; that they all mean essentially the same thing ('Please do not touch'); and that to remain human and free we must play ball games wherever and whenever we want.

ROSE BOYT

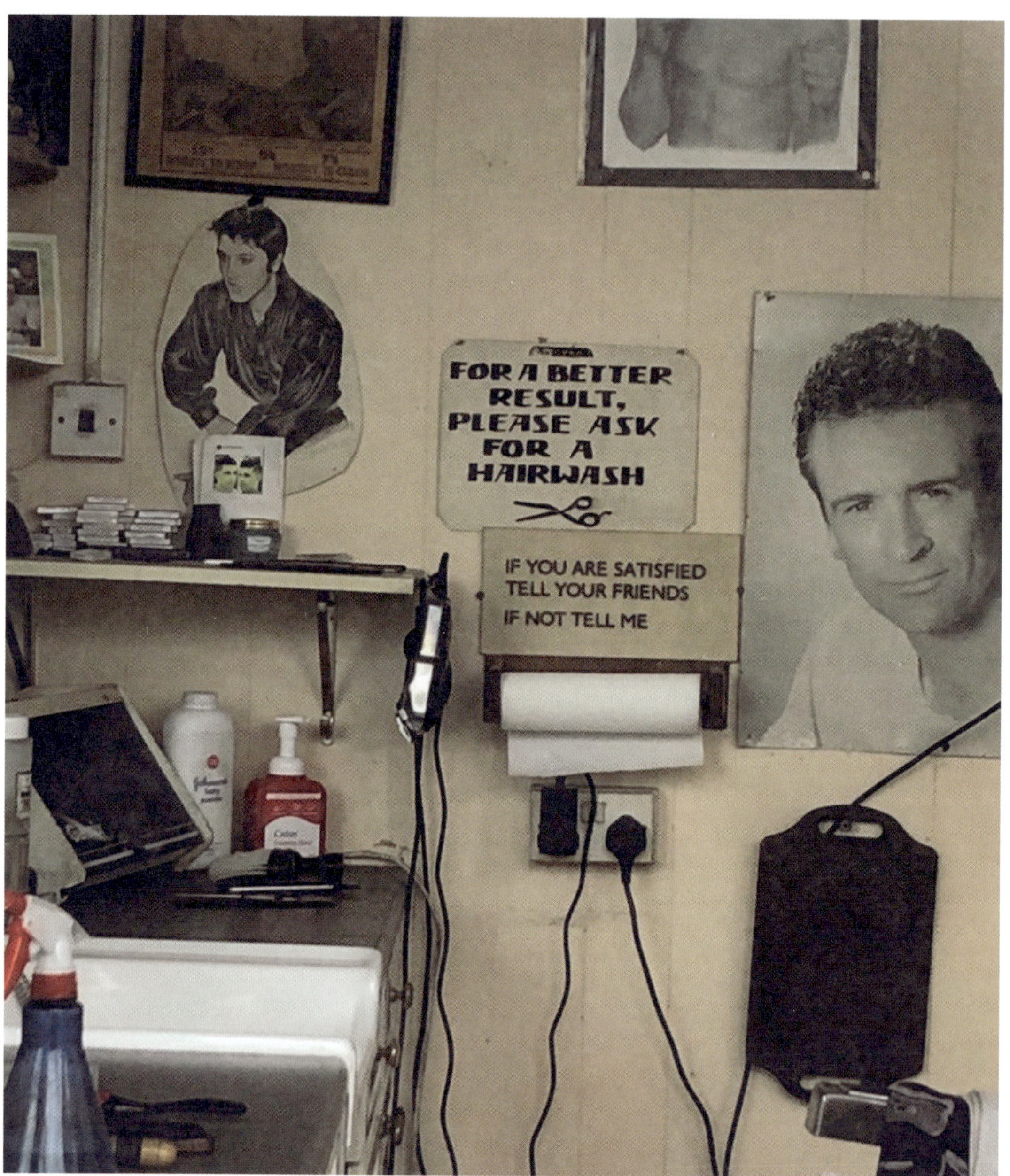

All our yesterdays.

STEVE FELDMAN

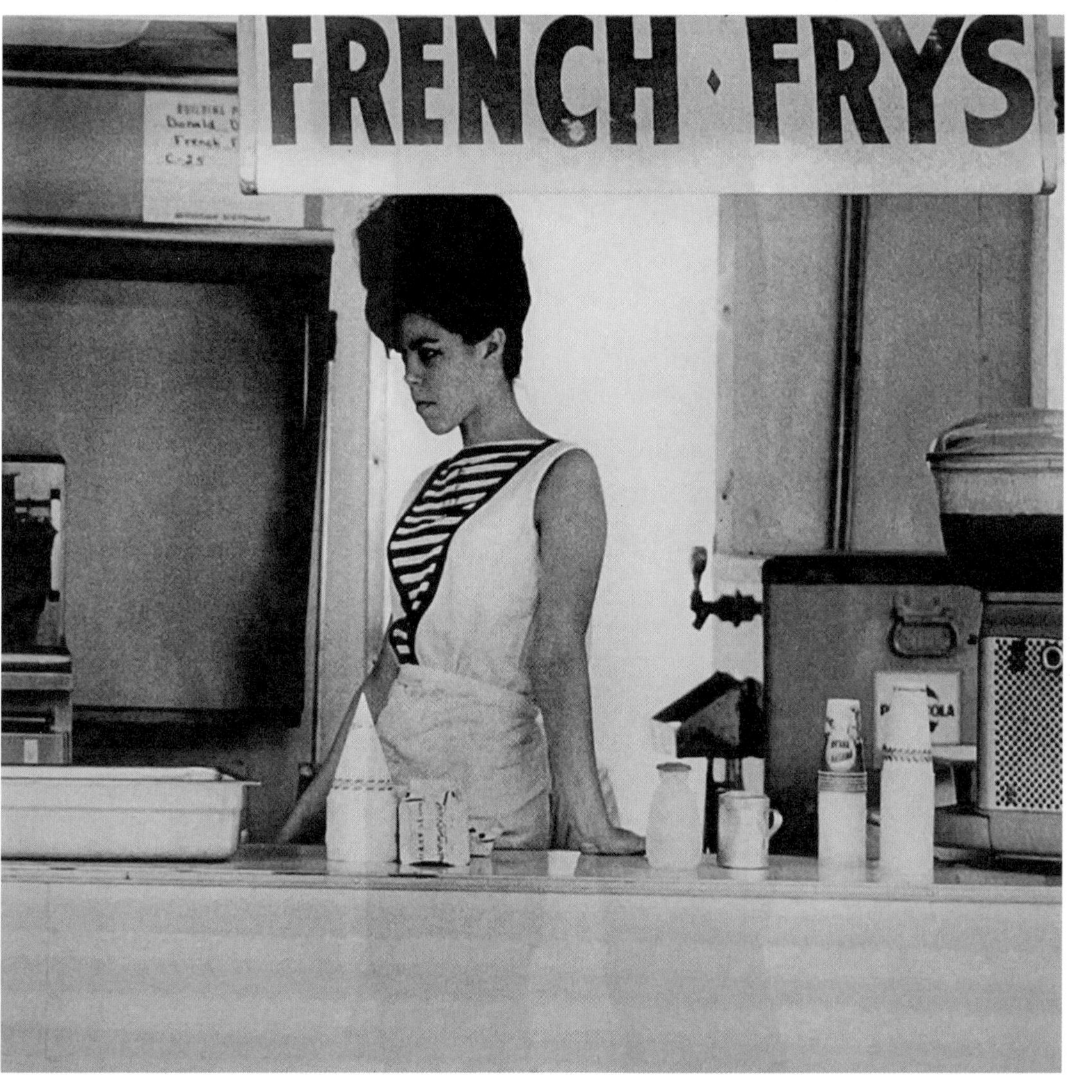

USA, 1960s.

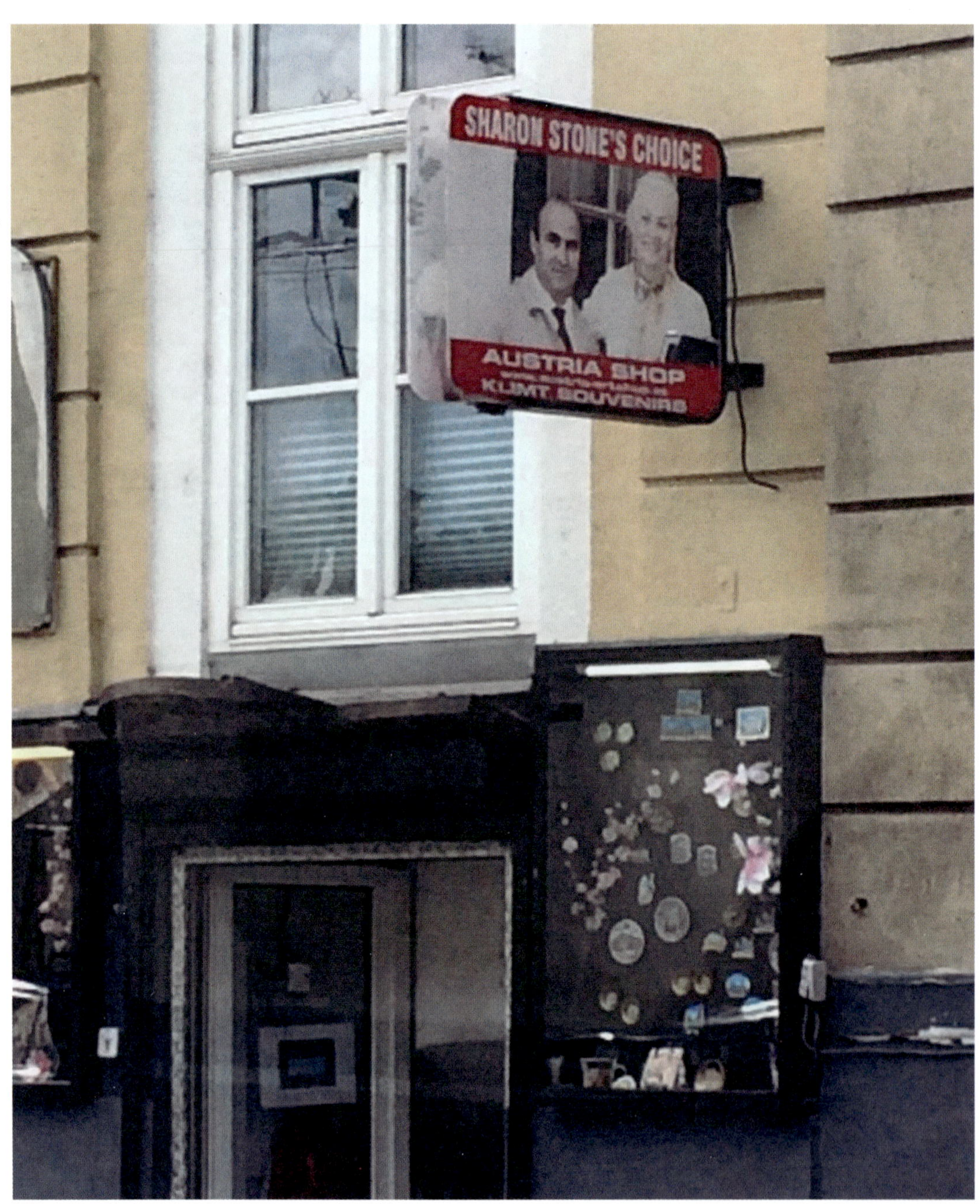

Sharon Stone's Choice, Vienna.

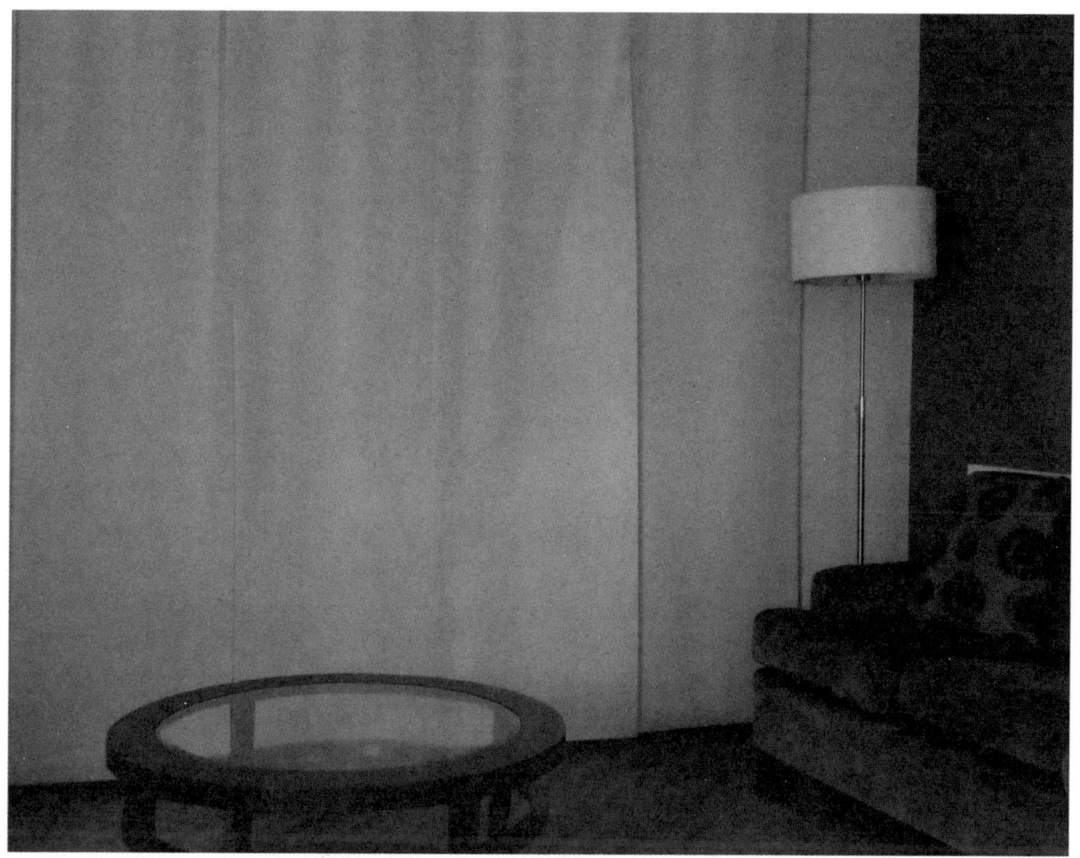

The last hotel room.

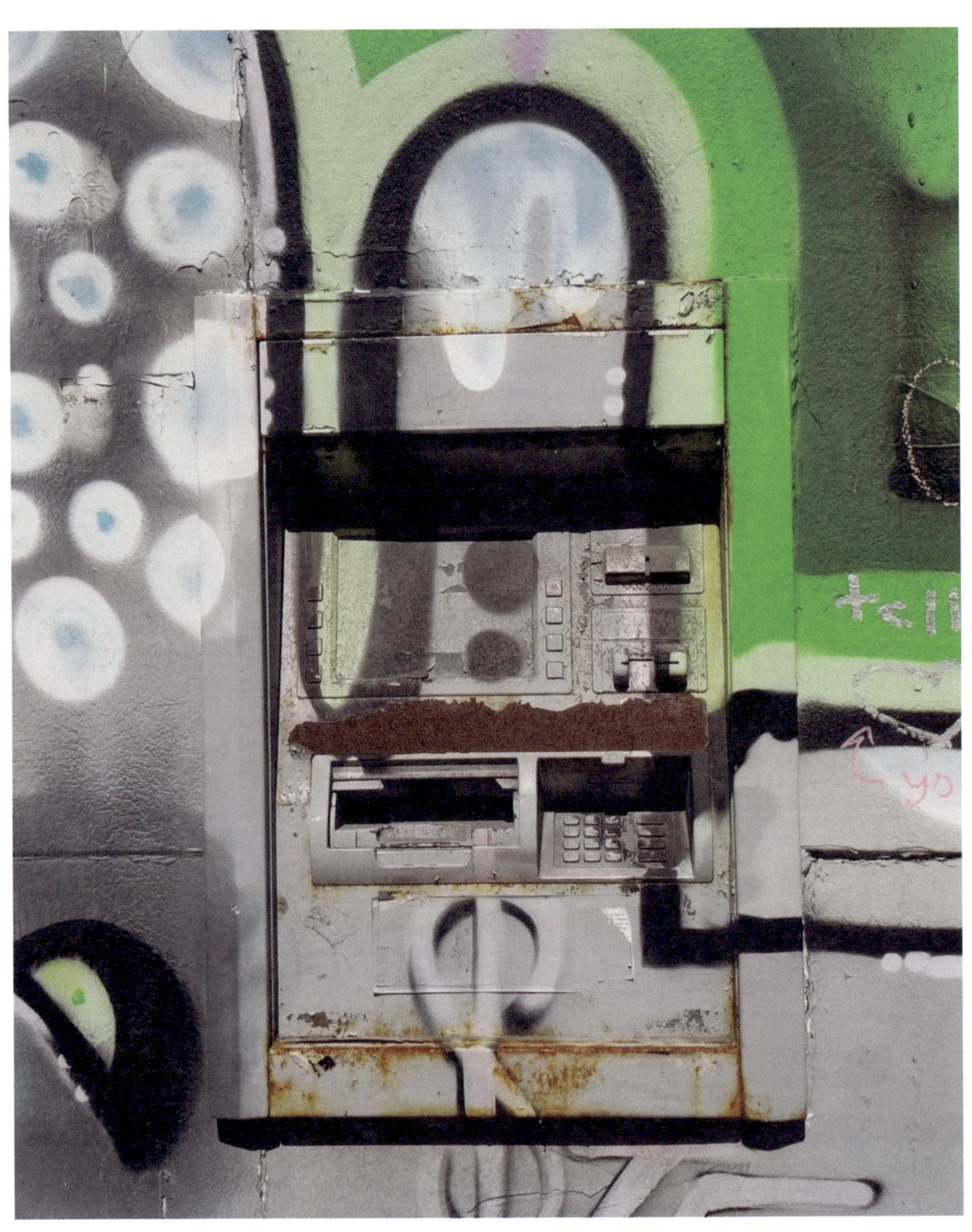

The colour of money.

3: preoccupations

AVEEK SEN

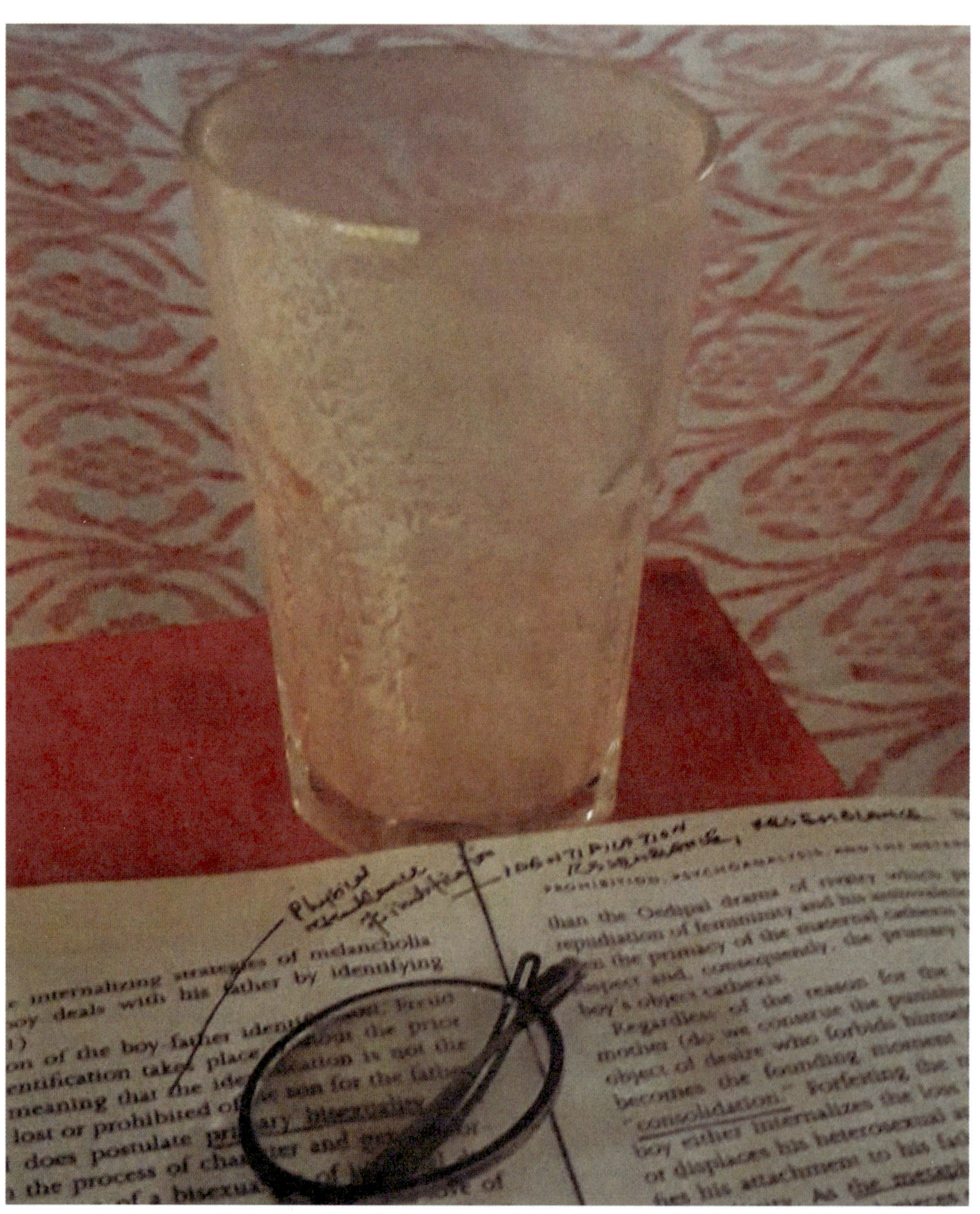
internalizing strategies of melancholia
boy deals with his father by identifying
than the Oedipal drama of
repudiation of femininity and his
Regardless of the reason for the
consolidation.

'WHAT DO YOU DO?' If I say I'm a writer, often there's a follow-up question: 'What else do you do?'

I used to make ships-in-bottles. I still make things: recently, worried that the UK was becoming a banana republic but couldn't even produce its own bananas, I made some bananas. Some people make cheese. A writer I published made tiny sculptures out of Edam cheese. A man who lived nearby made statues in his garden of Anglo-Irish historical figures, and indoors in the winter he made scale models of royal palaces. A lot of people enjoy gardening or birdwatching or knitting or mending old clocks. Some people are actually better at what they do on the side than at what they consider their main occupations.

Very many of these activities involve skill and close attention of a kind that automation has for centuries been rendering redundant. When particular professions are overtaken by technology – troubadours, cavalry officers, postilions, blacksmiths, compositors – particular ways of encountering and experiencing the world associated with those activities, mental ways along with the physical ways, may also vanish.

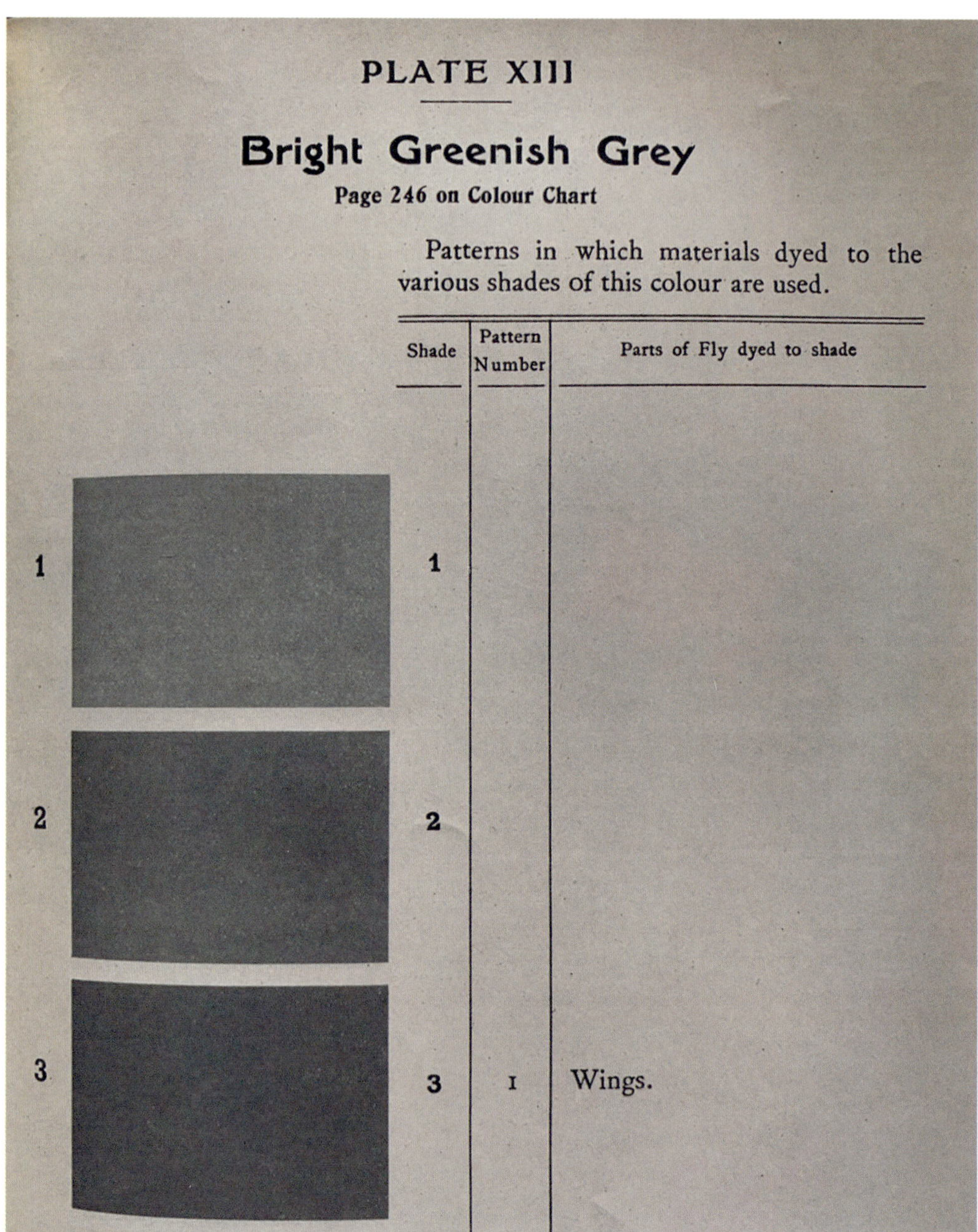

PLATE XIII

Bright Greenish Grey

Page 246 on Colour Chart

Patterns in which materials dyed to the various shades of this colour are used.

	Shade	Pattern Number	Parts of Fly dyed to shade
1	1		
2	2		
3	3	I	Wings.

Fly design covers many parameters: similitude in relation to natural insects, size, colour and hydrodynamic action – that is, how the fly is designed to move in the water. Frederic Halford's *Modern Development of the Dry Fly*, published in London in 1910, is one of the more iconic texts related to fly design.

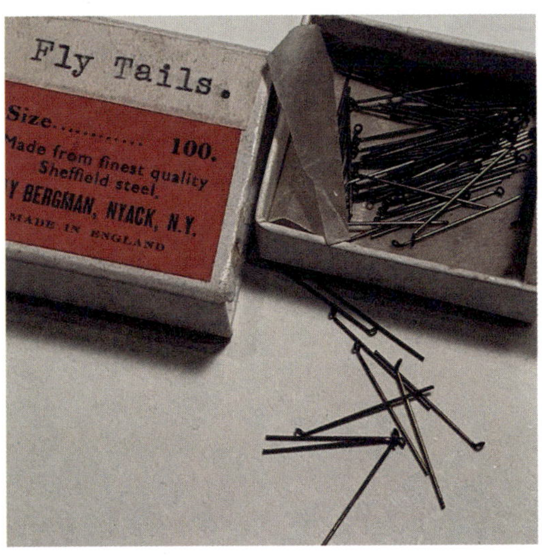

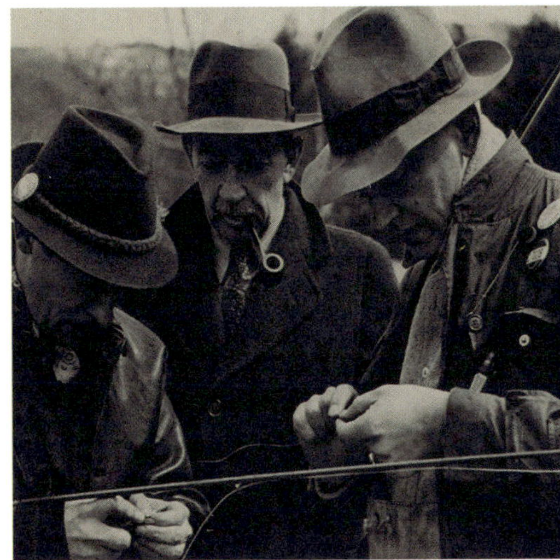

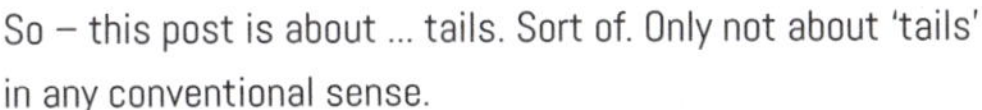

So – this post is about ... tails. Sort of. Only not about 'tails' in any conventional sense.
It's about fly tails and plum tails.
Fly tails. They consist of a hook eye and straight shank. No bend, no barb, no point. The eye is probably what you would find on a size 18 hook. These were sold by Ray Bergman, probably in the 1940s or early 1950s. Bergman was one of the premier angling authors in mid-century America. His books include *Just Fishing* (1932), *Trout* (1938), and *Fresh Water Bass* (1942). Bergman's expansive knowledge was irreproachable. Capitalizing on his reputation, he established himself as a retailer of fishing goods. However, Bergman's 1942 catalogue does not list 'Fly Tails.' The famous red-label box, which denoted his highest-quality hooks, would suggest they were especially prized, though their purpose is not clear.

Charles Ritz, Arnold Gingrich, and John Alden Knight streamside, probably late 1950s or early 1960s. I'm not sure where but it was close to NYC as Gingrich is still dressed for the office. Here's a favorite Labor Day quotation from Gingrich's book *The Joys of Trout* in a chapter on the famous angling author A. J. McClane: 'For twenty-five years Al McClane had an office, but it was one where, if he showed up, he was likely to be asked, "Why the hell aren't you out fishing?" For common mortals who have an office, when they don't show up there, but have been out fishing instead, the questions is, of course, "Where the hell have you been?" Obviously any man who can arrange to get that question reversed is just as much smarter as all the rest of us.' Happy Labor Day everyone.

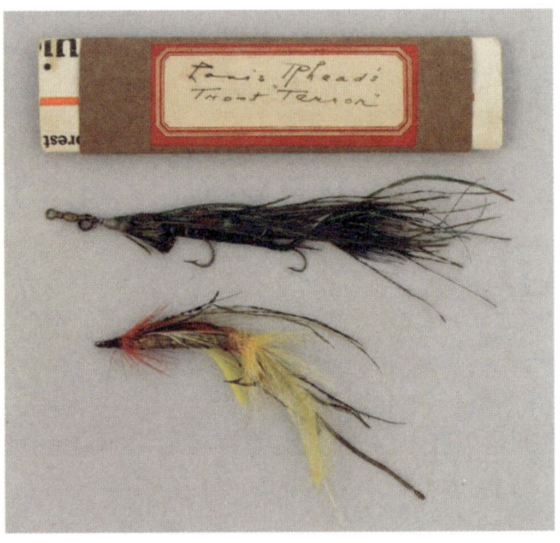

Louis Rhead (1857–1926) is perhaps one of the most unorthodox fly tiers ever – he was to fly tying what the 'mad' potter George Ohr was to ceramics. Born in England among a family of artists, Rhead was educated in Paris and developed a reputation as an illustrator of posters and children's books. In 1883 he emigrated to the US, and took up trout fishing shortly thereafter. He developed his own fly and lure patterns and sold them directly to the public. His best-known books include *American Trout Stream Insects: A Guide To Angling Flies and other Aquatic Insects Alluring to Trout* (1916) and *Fisherman's Lures and Game-Fish Food* (1920). Rhead died of a heart attack in 1926 when, after a long tussle with a 30-pound snapping turtle that had been pillaging his trout ponds, he collapsed on the shore and died.

JOSEPH GRIGELY

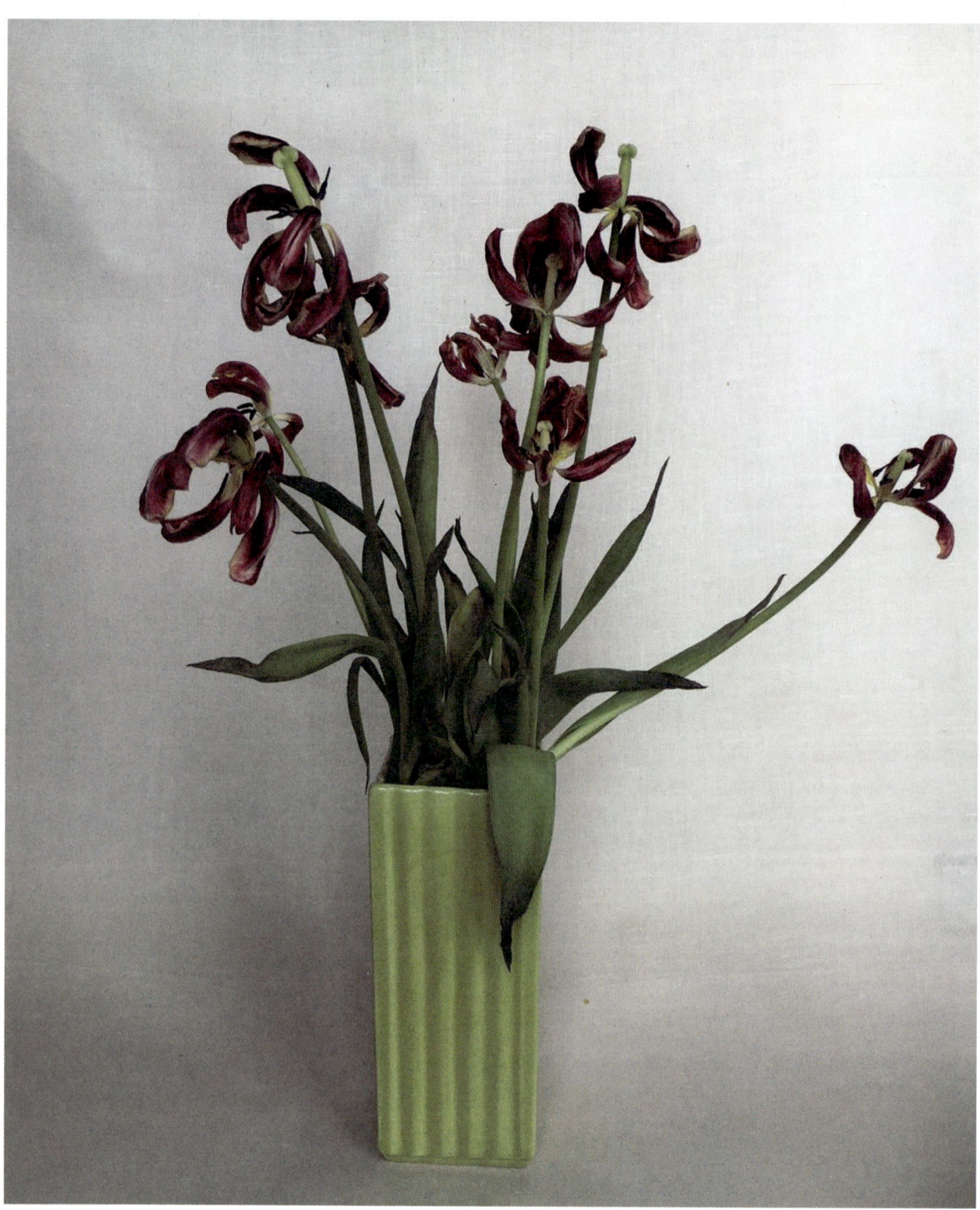

The last of the dead flowers, for now anyhow. The dead flowers idea in our house belongs to Amy Vogel, who for most of the 20-odd years I have known her has explored in her work the difficulty of beauty. The phrase actually comes from the wonderful plant magician, Paula Hayes, who, one day, was telling me a story about a blind baby who imitated, perfectly, the sound of the refrigerator and the sound of a car coming up a gravel driveway. 'Beauty is difficult,' Paula said to me. 'Never forget that.'

JOSEPH GRIGELY

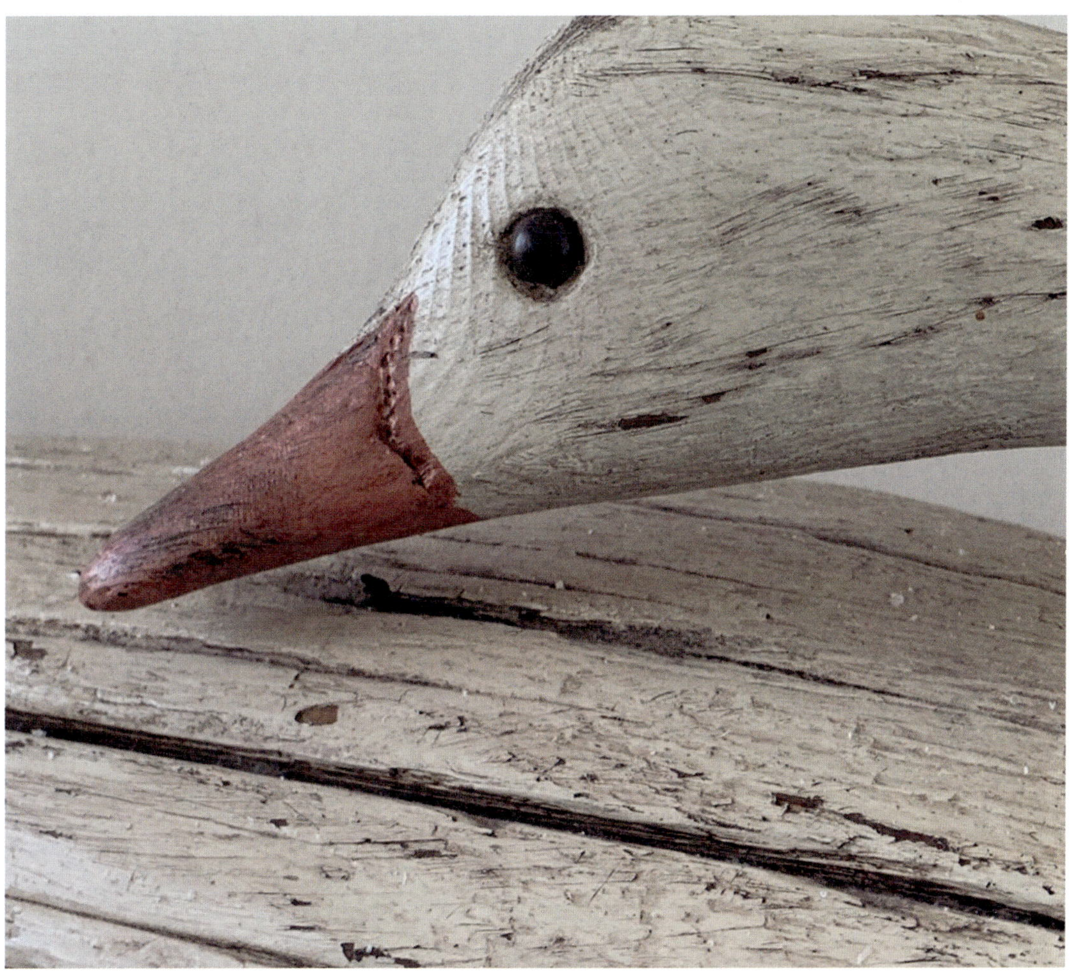

Six ducks, a coot, a swan, a loon, and a goose: decoys from Roger Brown's collection, New Buffalo, Michigan. Decoys play an important role in the history of representing nature. In the process of being made (by an artisan) and then being used (by a hunter), they take nature from outside to inside, where it is reshaped and remade, and then taken outside again where decoys are employed with the task of deception – fooling birds into believing they are the real thing.

Not all decoys were made to be used; many were carved as an art form, and the auction prices reflect it: several have sold in the range of $500,000–$800,000. Brown mostly paid between $50–$100 for his decoys, which he found in antique shops in the 1980s. Most were made from pine and cedar. More than being quaint curiosities of a bygone time, Brown's collection of decoys reflects an idiosyncratic way in which he collected different creative practices as a way of influencing his own. He liked stuff that was outside the norm of the art world's inside: wood sculptures from Africa, slipware pottery, Navajo blankets, Howard Finster's texts and assemblages, Russel Wright dinnerware. Much of the work Brown collected was emphatically hand-made: it's *slow art*.

In a world like ours, where doing more, and doing it faster, is becoming the modus operandi, it is a relief to find meaning in doing things slow, and doing things in an understated way.

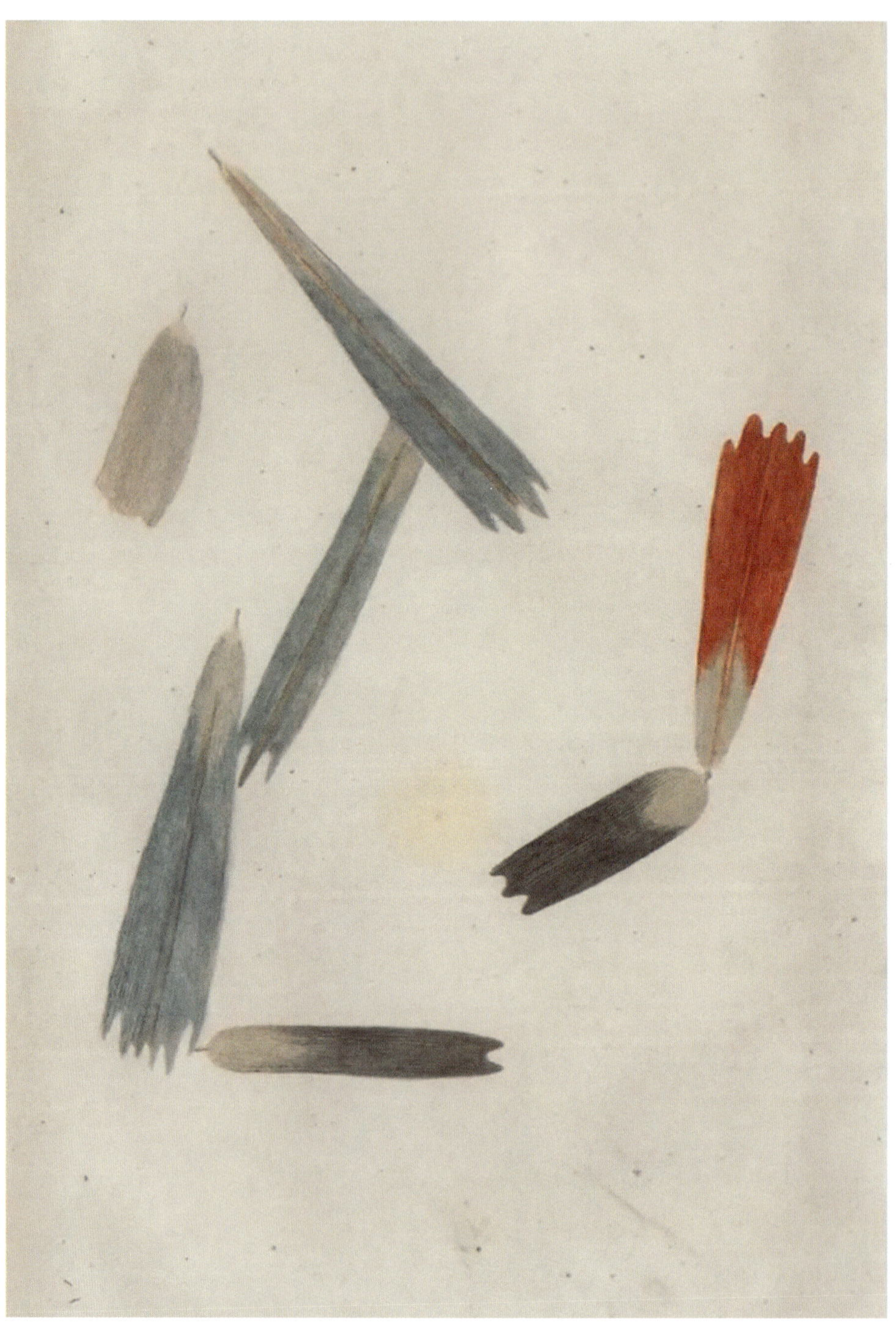

Ernst Heeger (Austrian, 1783–1866), 'Catocala nupta. Squamae alae.', 1860, Hand-coloured salt print, 20.3 x 13.6 cm. These are the wing scales of a red underwing moth as captured by Heeger's solar microscope and coloured by hand.

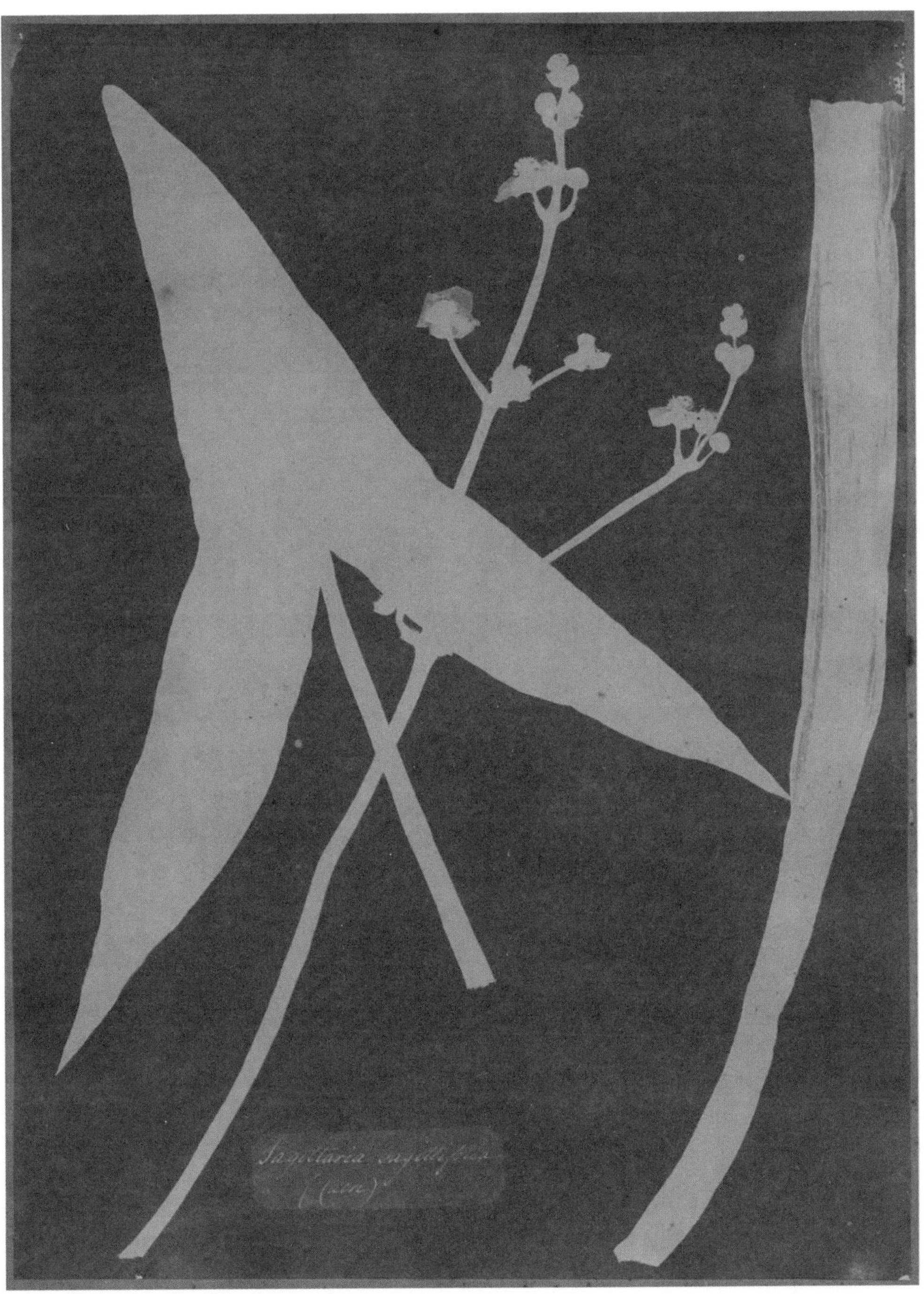

Anna Atkins (English, 1799–1871),'Sagittaria sagittifolia,' 1851-1854, Cyanotype photogram, 34.6 x 24.6 cm. This one shows the flowering arrowhead plant, and is a striking precursor of the expressive photography of twentieth century and contemporary artists.

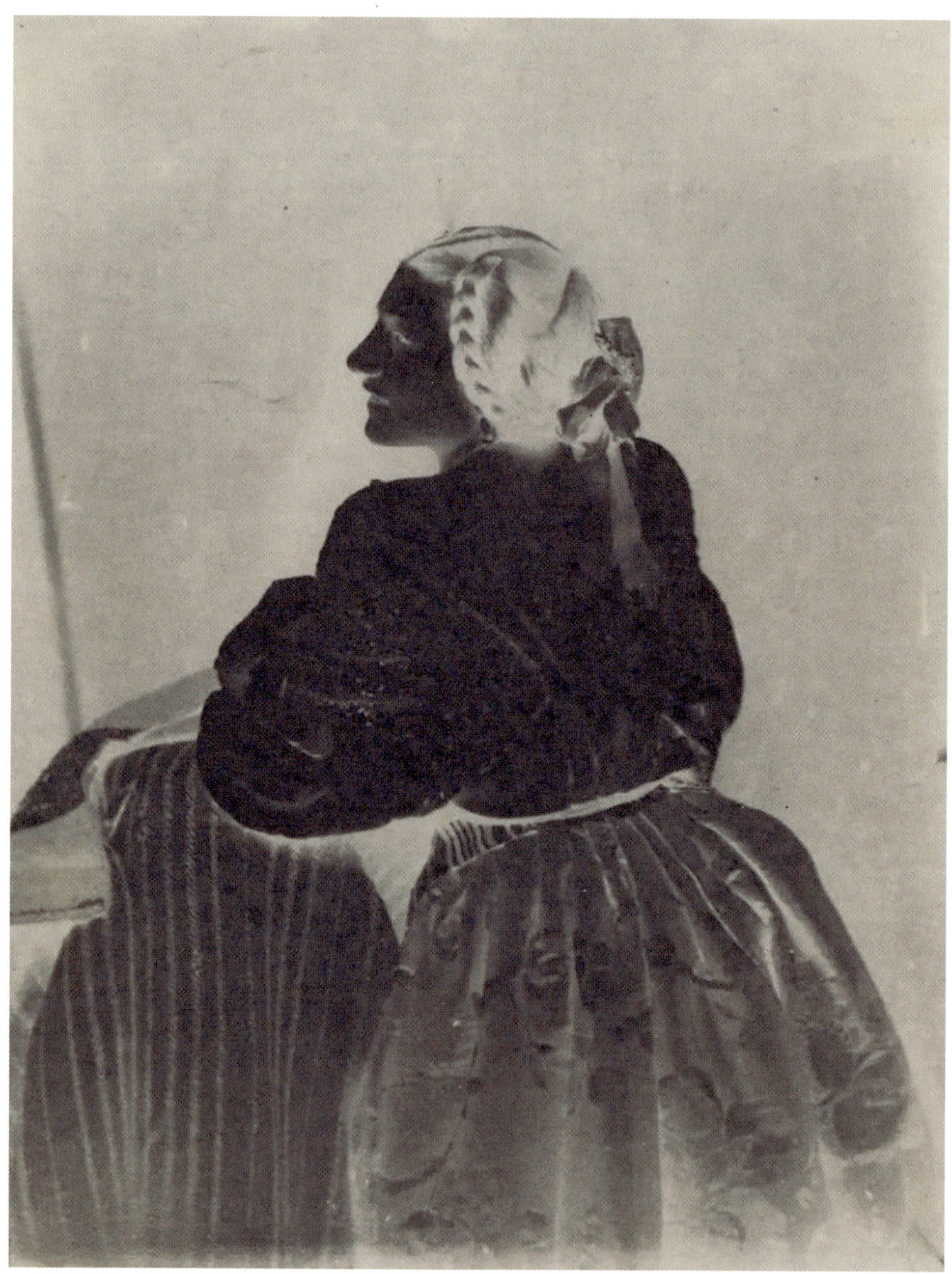

Julien Vallou de Villeneuve (French, 1795–1866), *Woman with braid*, c.1852, paper negative, 16.5 x 13.0 cm. Vallou de Villeneuve was a French painter, lithographer and photographer. His photographic works are most closely associated with the painter Gustave Courbet who, during the 1850s, used many of Vallou's photographs as source material for his paintings.

HANS KRAUS

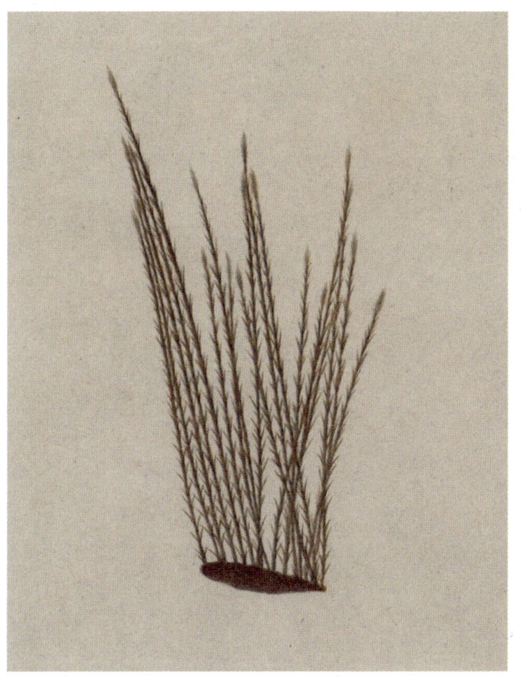

Ernst Heeger (Austrian, 1783–1866), *Abdominal hairs of a honey bee*, 1861, Hand-coloured salt print, 20.2 x 13.5 cm. Heeger's photomicrograph affords us this close-up view of the branched posterior hairs of the honey bee. The hairs capture pollen and help pollinate the lovely spring flowers we all of us look forward to seeing after a long winter.

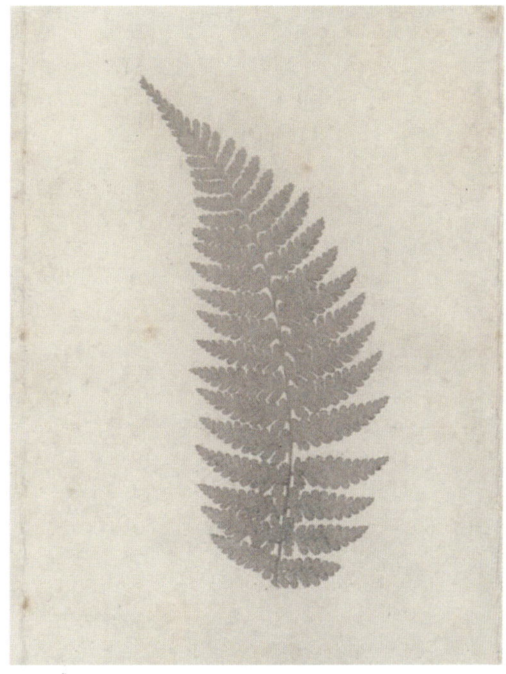

William Henry Fox Talbot (English, 1800–1877) *Fern*, circa 1852, Photographic engraving, 20.3 x 12.8 cm. This simple photographic engraving experiment of a single fern conveys in a permanent print Talbot's original vision for his invention. It is one of his earliest examples of the photogravure.

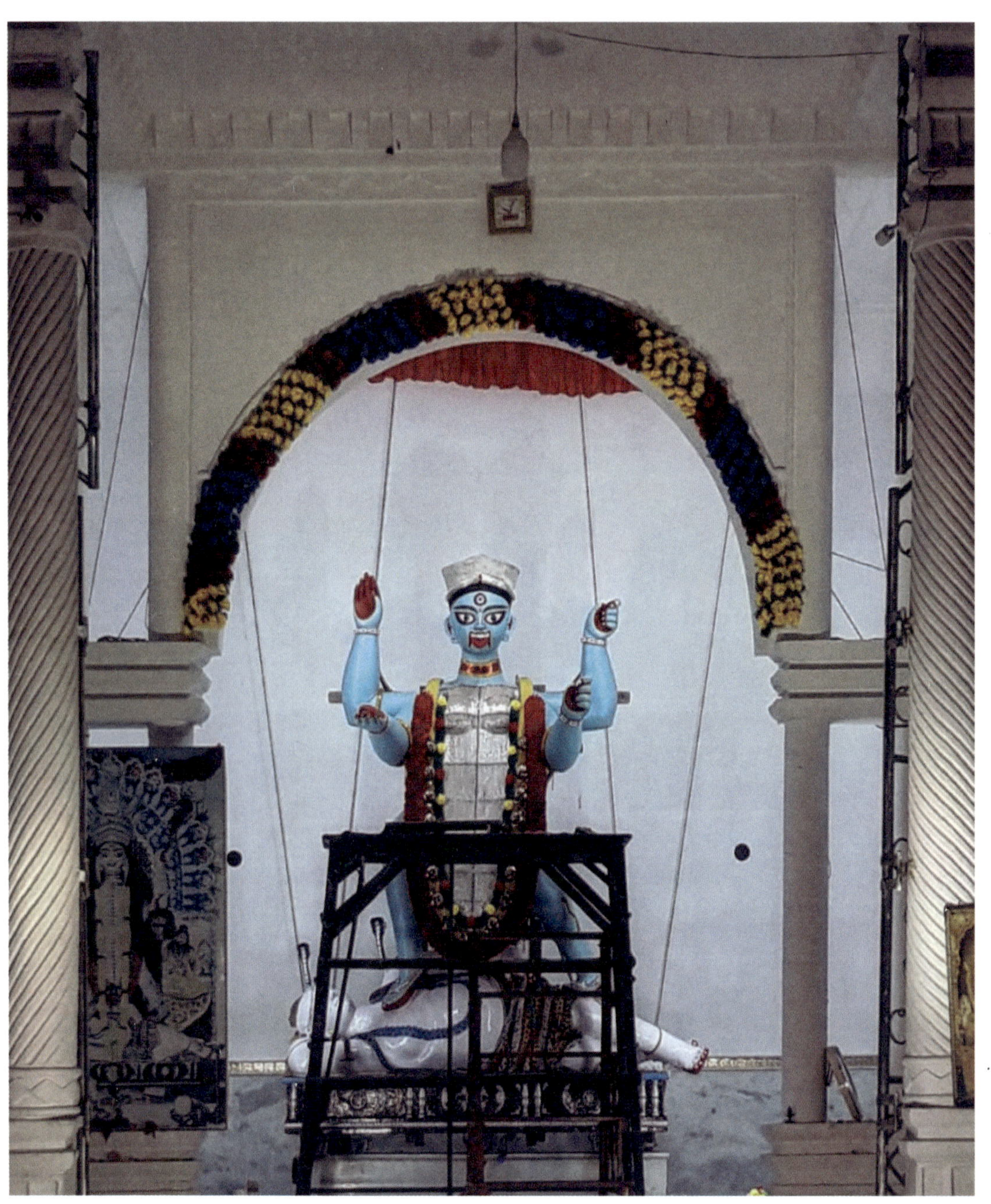

AVEEK SEN

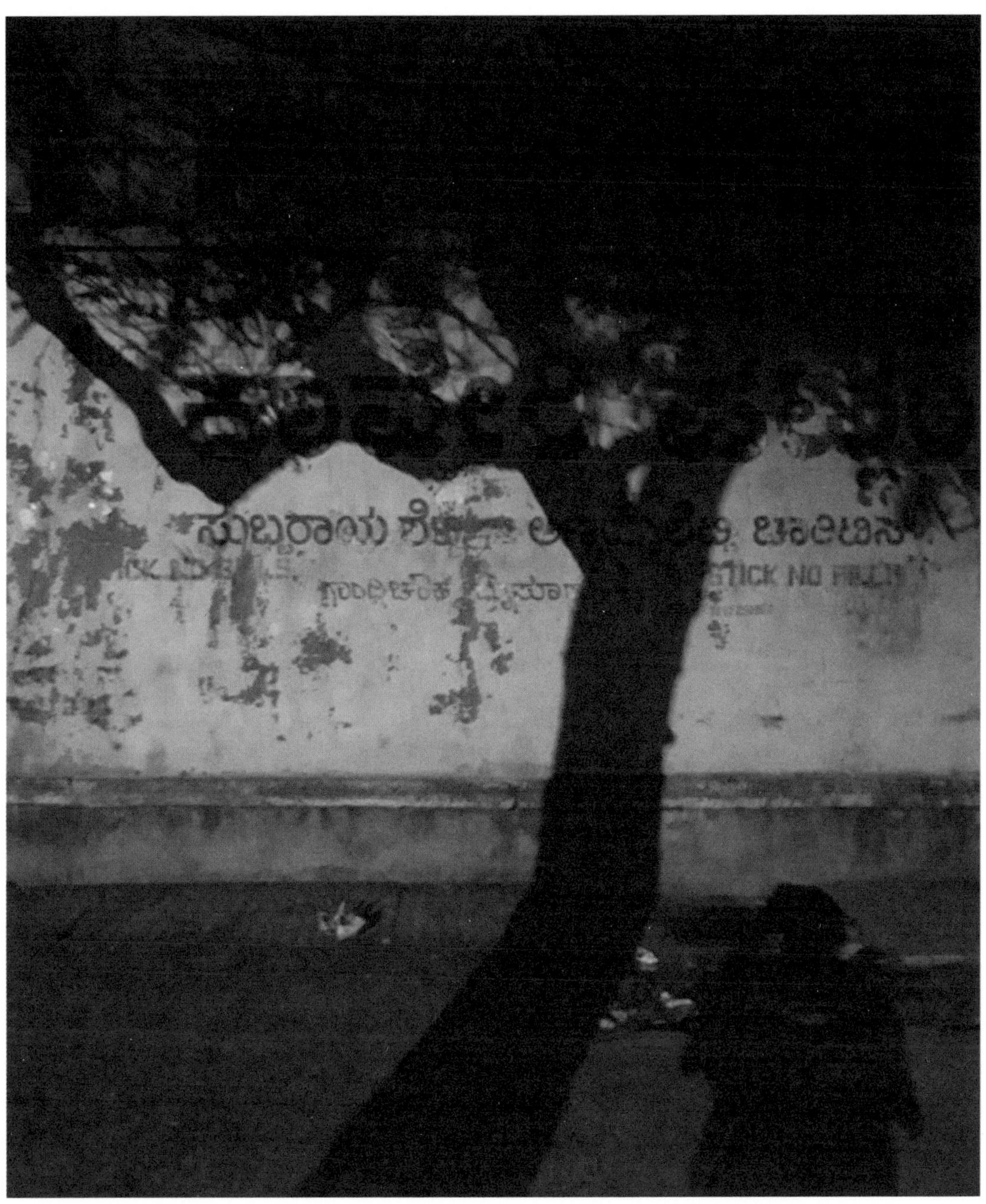

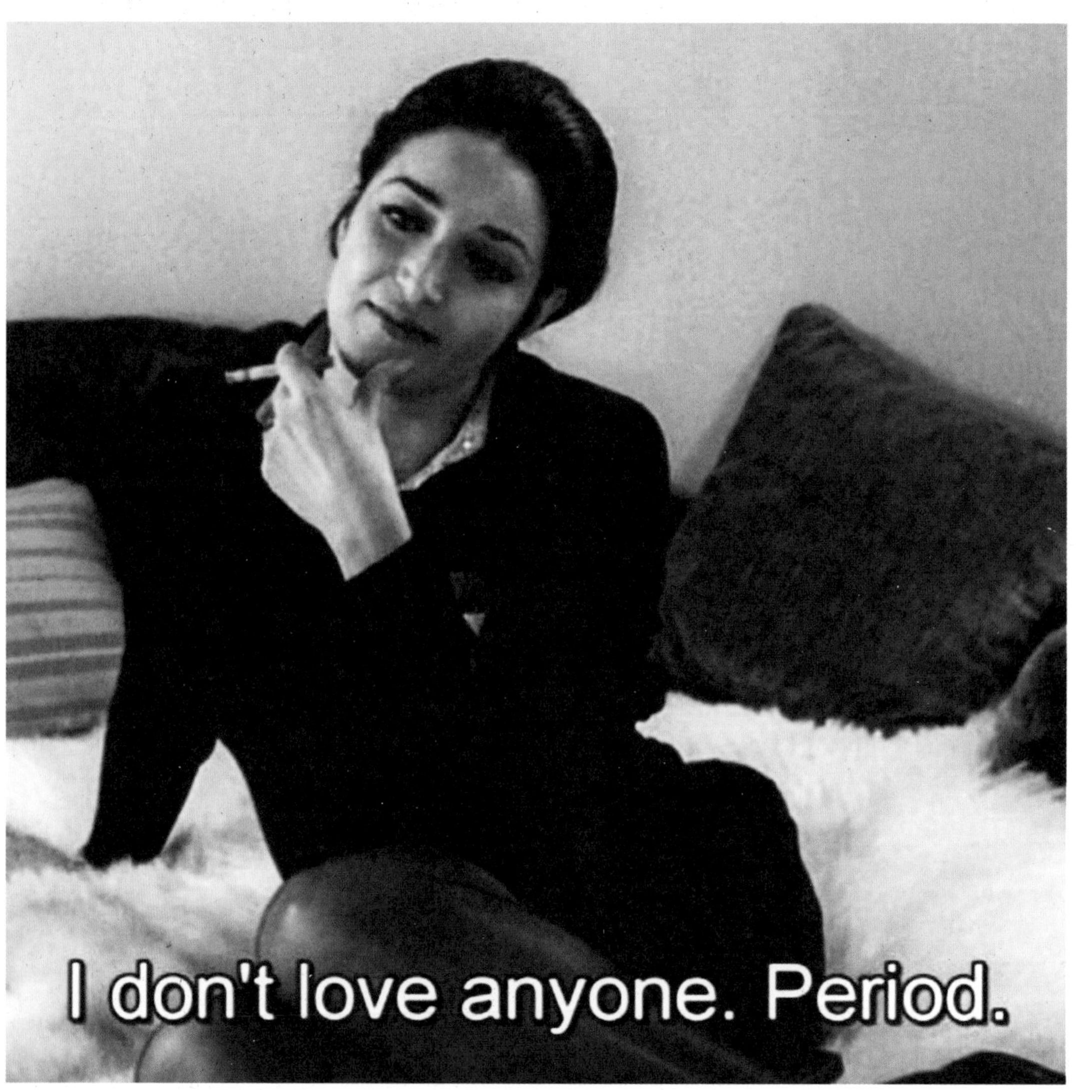
I don't love anyone. Period.

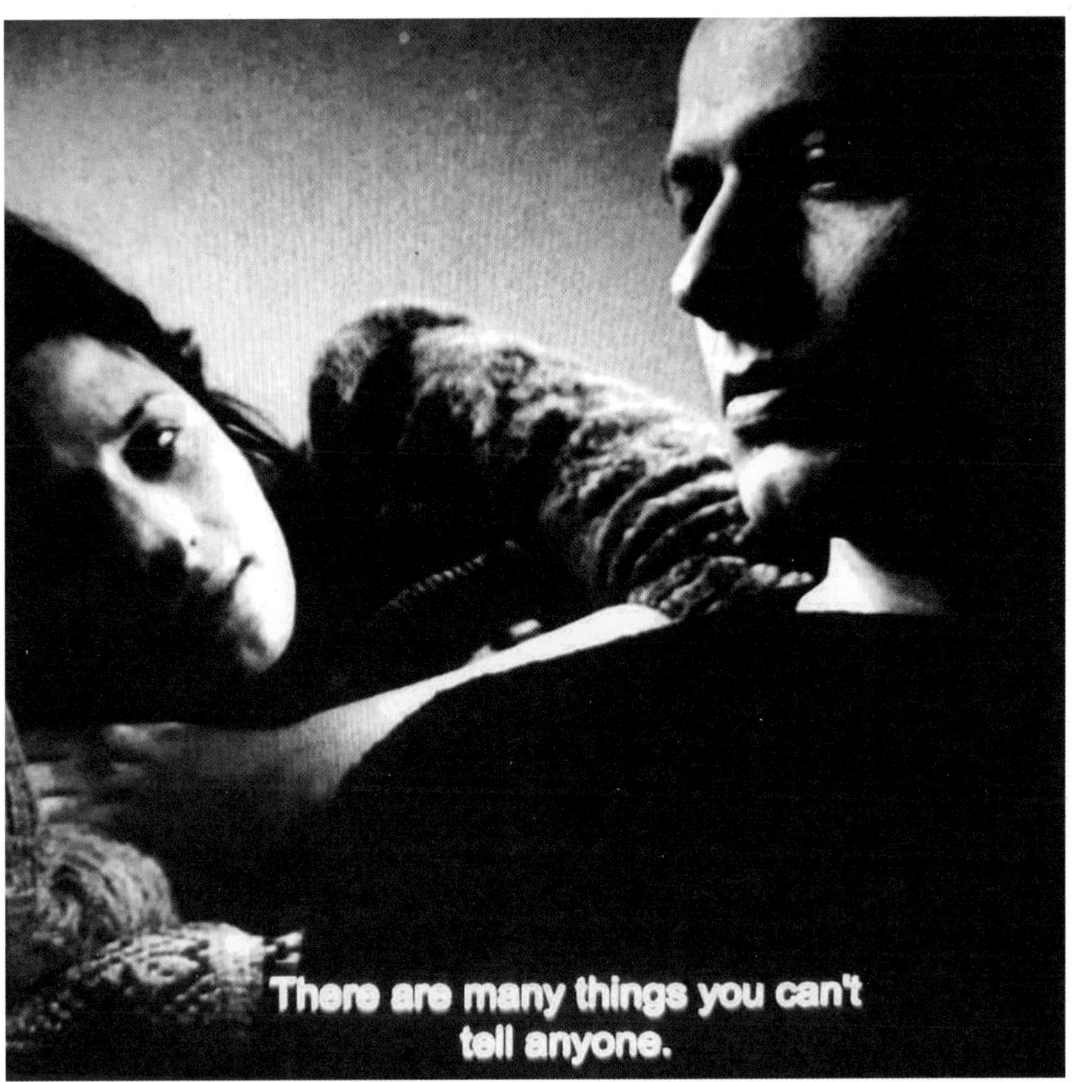
There are many things you can't
tell anyone.

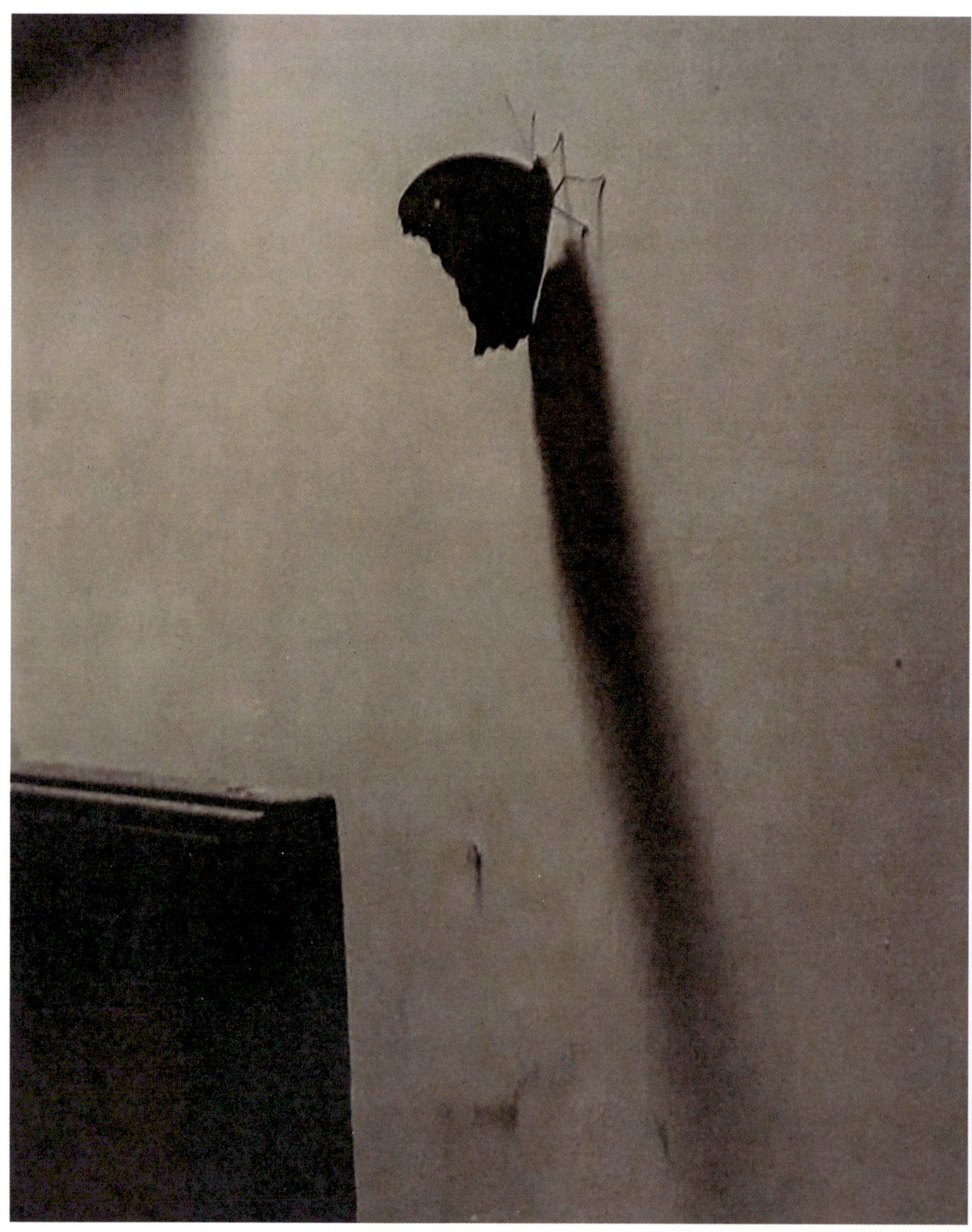

AVEEK SEN

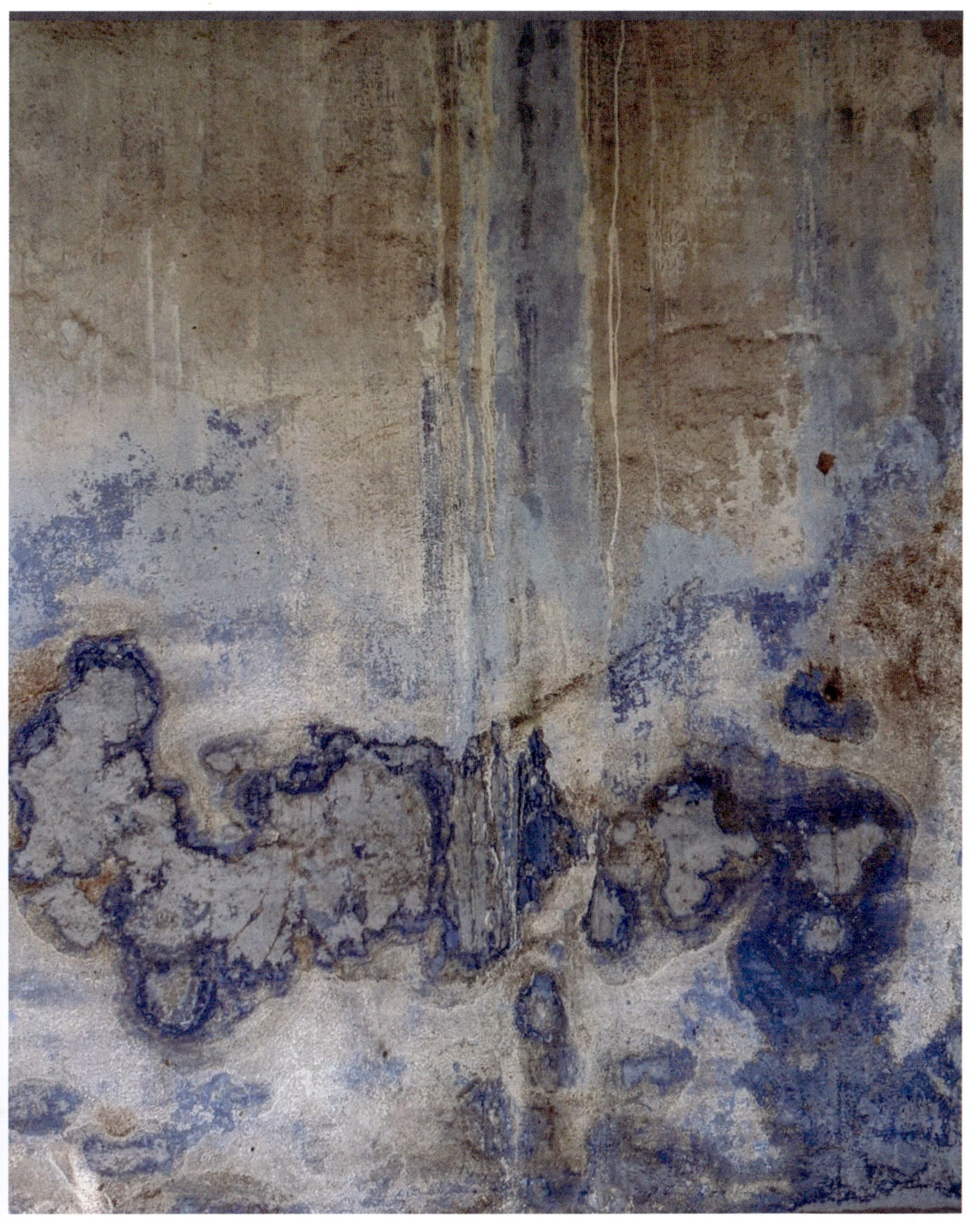

ARADHANA SETH

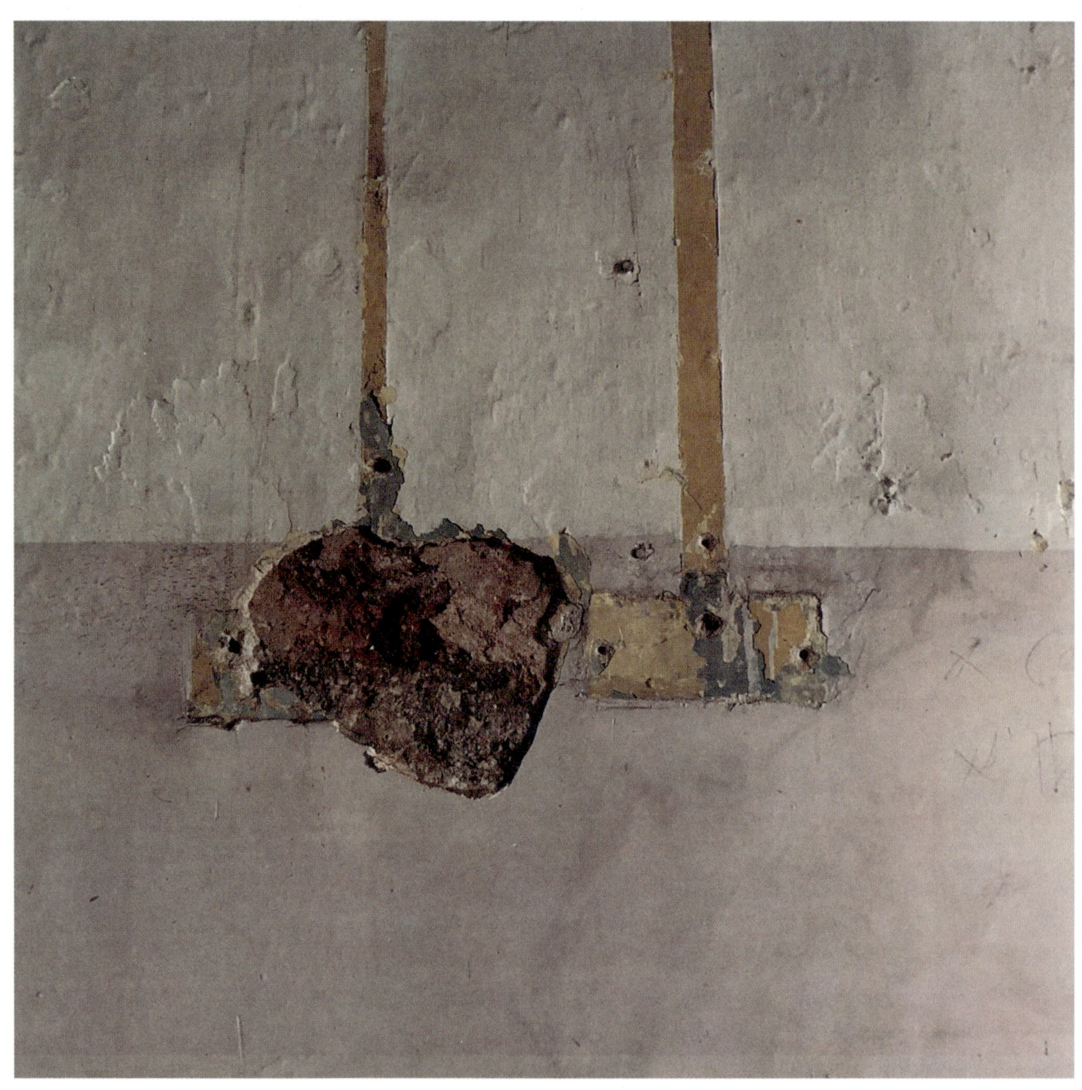

4: discoveries

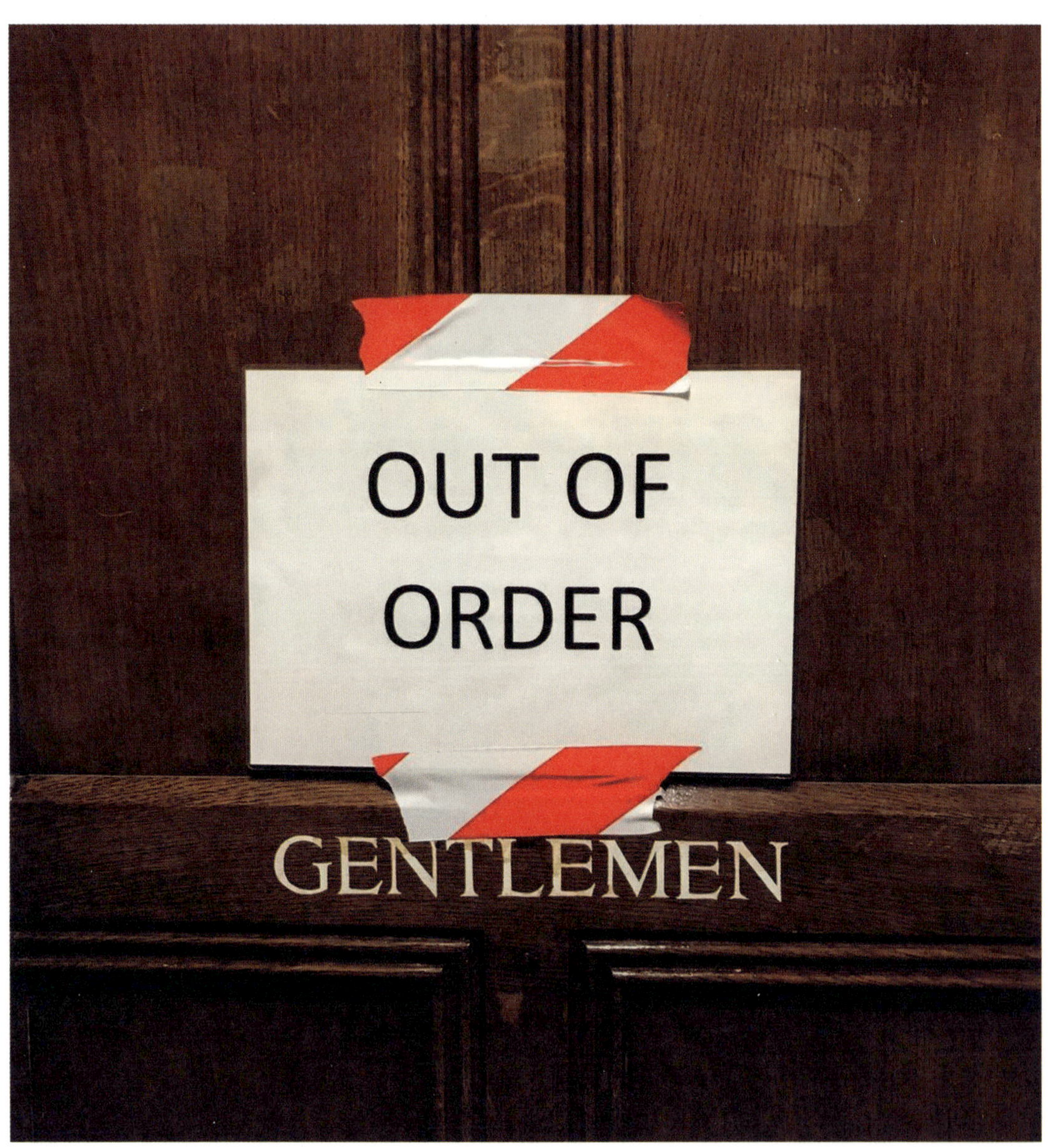
OUT OF
ORDER
GENTLEMEN

CAREY YOUNG

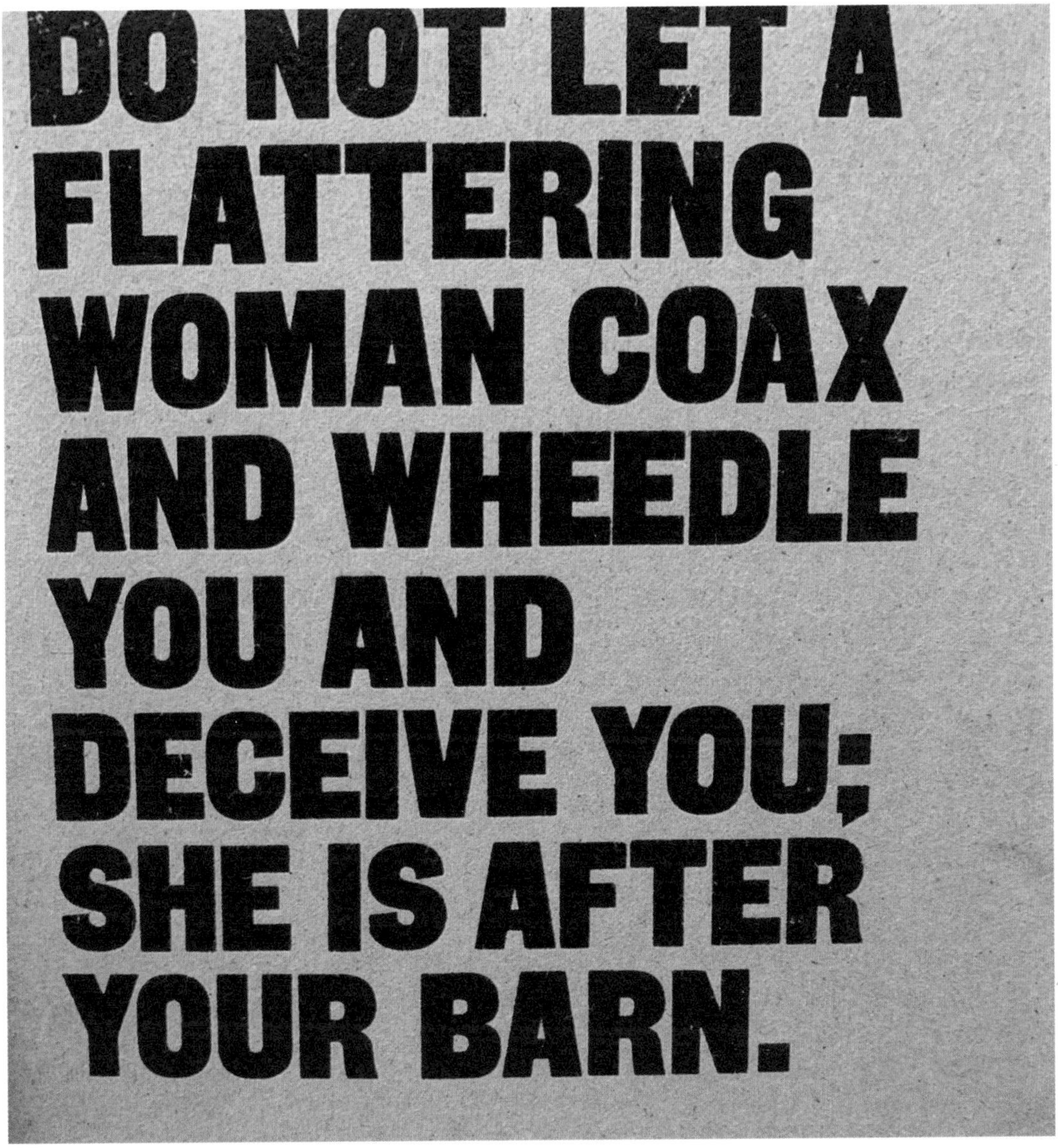

DO NOT LET A FLATTERING WOMAN COAX AND WHEEDLE YOU AND DECEIVE YOU; SHE IS AFTER YOUR BARN.

A quote by Hesiod (650–750 BC)

BAD TIMING WHILE CROSSING THE ROAD and you can end up in hospital in a coma. More bad timing, wrong accent, a face that fits, and you can be put away for a crime you didn't commit ... That man who hadn't got the right paperwork and was stuck in Charles de Gaulle airport for 18 years. That soldier who didn't get the message that Japan had surrendered at the end of World War Two and who hid out in the jungle in the Philippines for 29 years. What the precise numbers indicate is the banality of interruptions. I assume, of course, that at some never-precisely-dated point the interrupted life becomes simply the life as lived, and that the arrival of correct paperwork for man-in-airport, or news of end of hostilities for man-in-jungle, would have come as a secondary interruption, to be resisted.

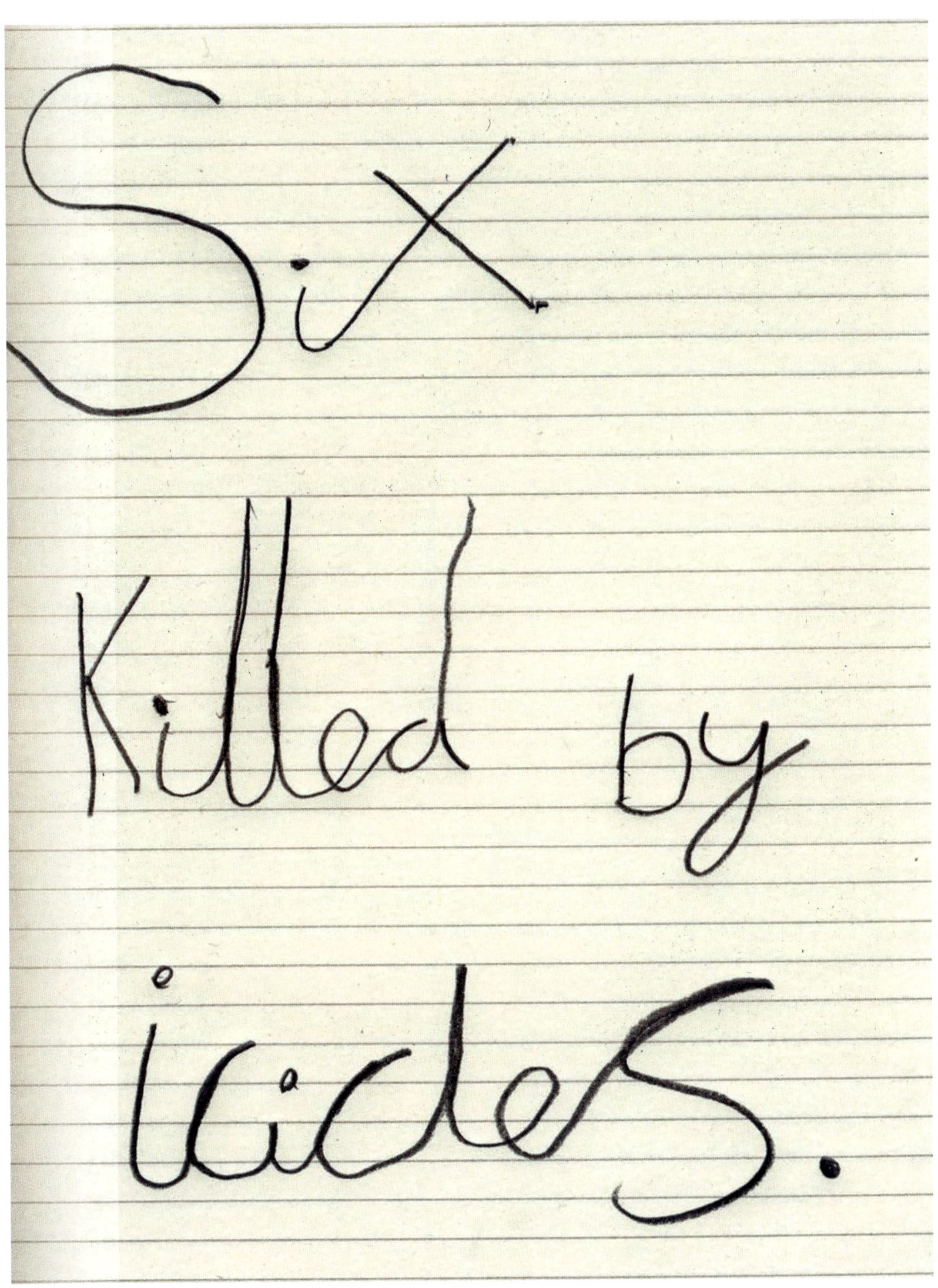

Six Killed by Icicles 2008. News headline copied by my (then) 7-year-old daughter.

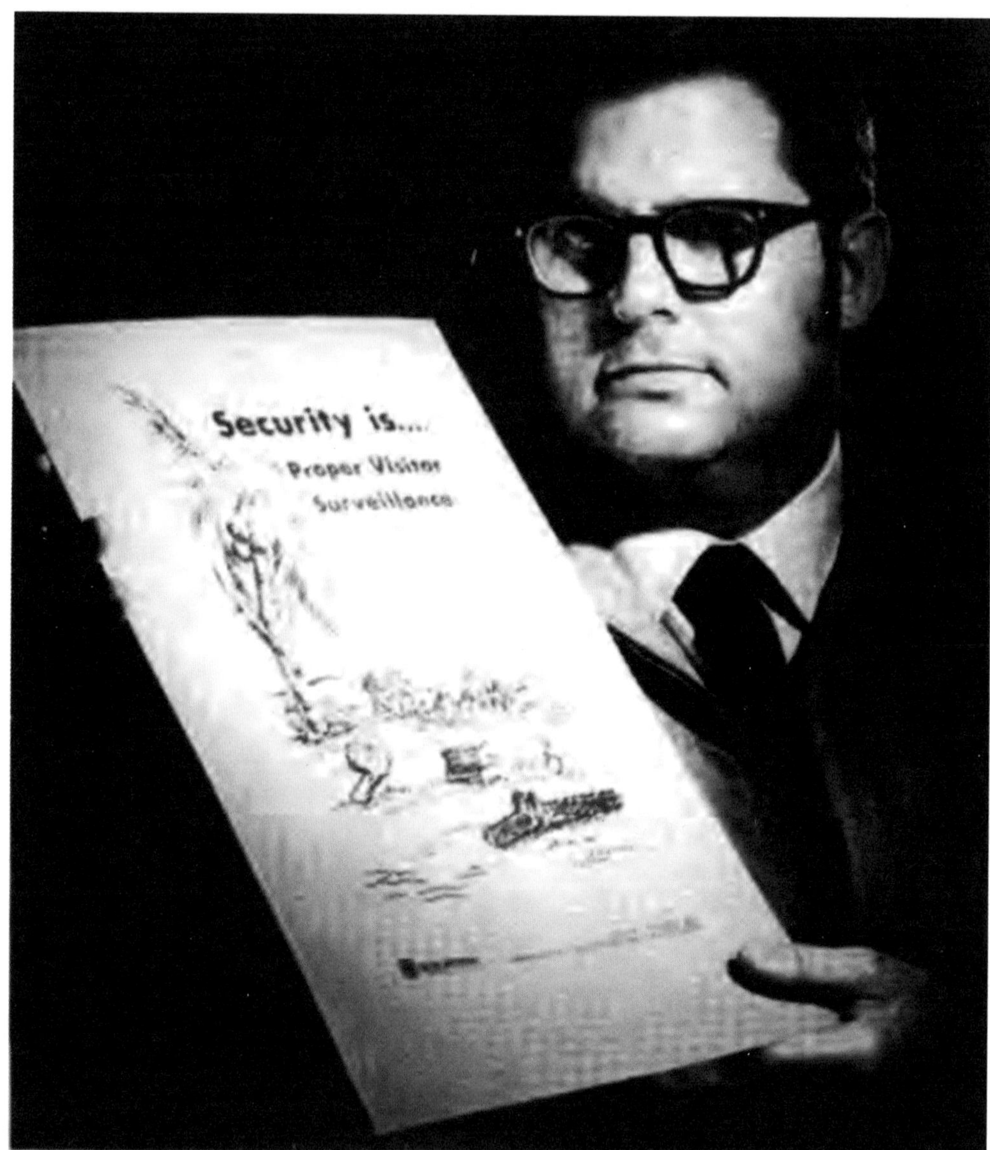

"SECURITY IS" CONTEST—Tom Grayson (8254) submitted the winning caption for June, "Security is Proper Visitor Surveillance."

Tom's dinner parties are sometimes tense.

GLEN BAXTER

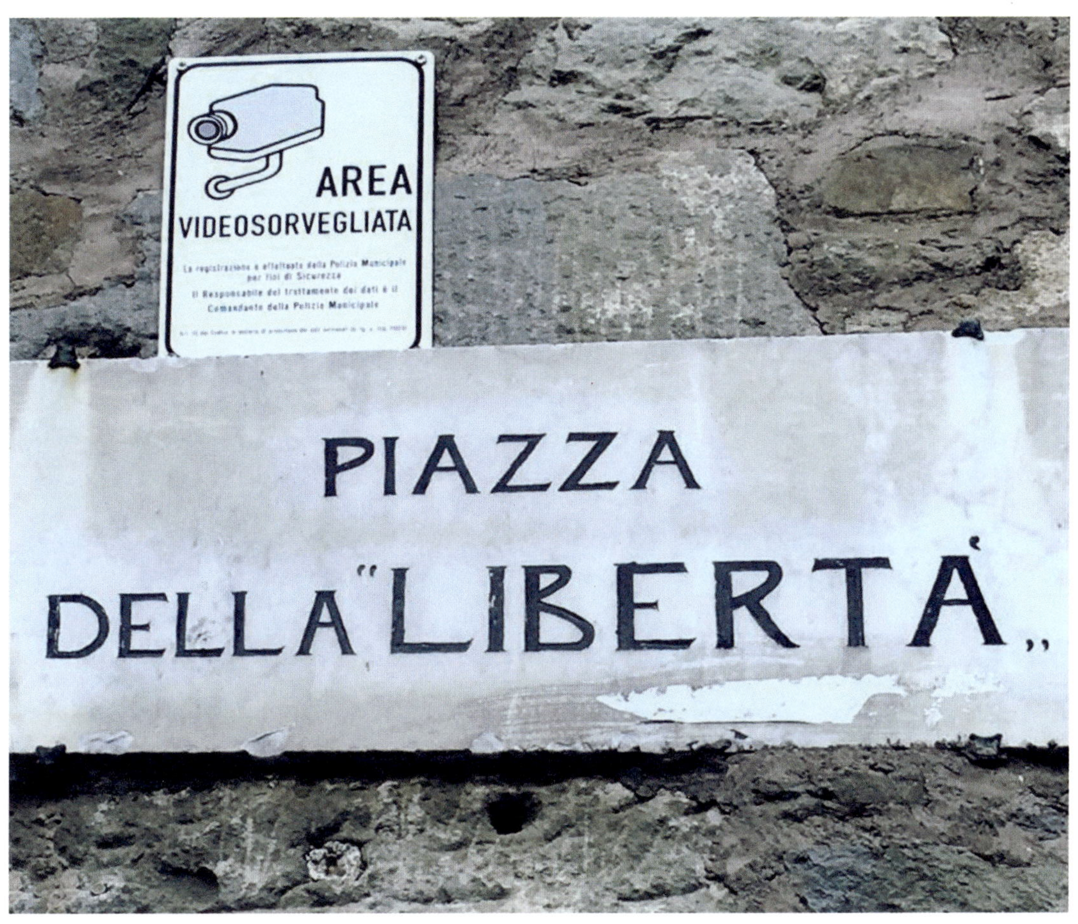

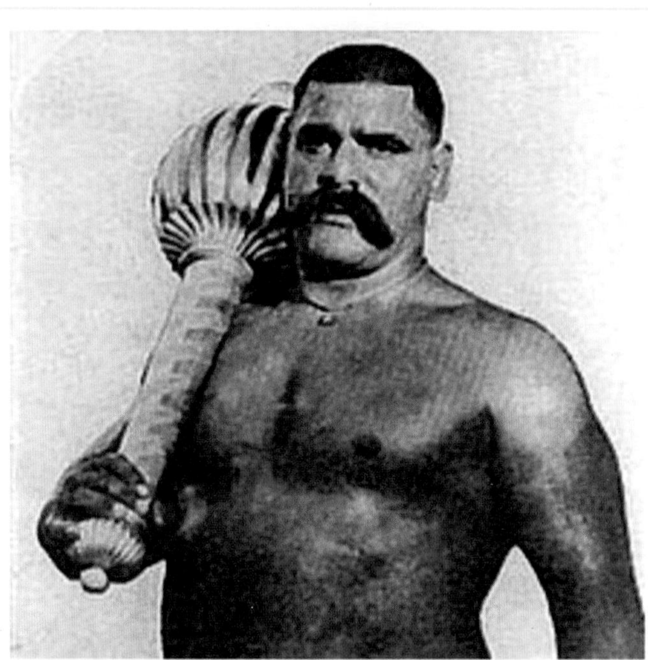

Birth name	Ghulam Mohammad Baksh Butt[1]

When I was small, I absorbed a great number of references that my parents made to things I'd never seen or experienced, and would, in many cases, never see or experience. Some of this was about Sylhet, where they grew up – its food, schools, families, cultural events, even its toilets. Some of it was about people obscure to me but significant to them. One of them was Gama. Whenever my mother wished to express her startlement at how imposing a person was, she'd say, 'O dekhi Gamar mato!' or 'I see he's just like Gama!' I wasn't sure if gama was a thing or person. Or, if someone had put on weight: 'Ekta Gama hoye jachhe!' or 'They're becoming a Gama!' The 'a' or 'ekta' deepened my confusion about what gama was. I heard, too, that when I was an infant and feeding ferociously on my mother's milk and growing in size, my uncle would say, 'Eta Gama hoye gechhe!' The term was always used with a mixture of affection and awe. In the early years of this millennium, my mother used it lovingly of a nephew's daughter when she was a toddler (just as she called my daughter 'bombete' or 'pirate' when she was a child for all her frenetic daily preoccupations) – not even 'like Gama'; she just addressed her as 'Gama' until she had to be gently reminded that her great-niece had a name. Over time, I became vaguely aware that Gama was perhaps a wrestler of yore, but he remained a shadowy figure in comparison to the various prototypes my mother identified in the world around us. So it was with joy that I found, through Google, that today is the great man's birthday, and I'm delighted to see, for the first time, what he looked like.

Bāwar-chī phir nashe mẽ hai,	the cook is drunk again
Ṣāḥib kā mizāj āj bahut garm hai,	the Ṣāḥib is in a bad temper to-day.
Shorbe mẽ kuchh maza nahī̃, phīkā hai.	the soup has no taste, it is insipid.
Kharch āmadanī se do-gunā hai,	my expenditure is double my income.
Agar tujhe apnī jān 'azīz hai, to merī bāt sun,[1]	if you value your life [as of course you do], then listen to me.[1]
Golī mere sir ke ūpar ūpar chalī ga,ī	the bullet passed just over my head (all the way).
Ham tum-ko bẽt khilā,ẽge,	I will have you caned.
Yih kuttā sā nā-pāk jān-war tum ne kahā̃ se pāyā?	whence did you obtain this dog-like unclean animal?
Yih wuhī billī hai jo kal yahā̃ thī,	this is the same cat that was here yesterday.
Tum ne bakrī ko kyū̃ ghar mẽ āne diyā?	why did you allow the goat to come into the house?
Yih pagṛī tum ko ach-chhī nahī̃ lagtī.	this turban does not suit you.

Completely love this. Everything you need to know about the Raj in one page from an 1890s anthology of useful Hindustani phrases. Hard to choose a favourite but either *The cook is drunk again, The bullet just passed over my head* or *Why did you allow the goat to come into my house?*

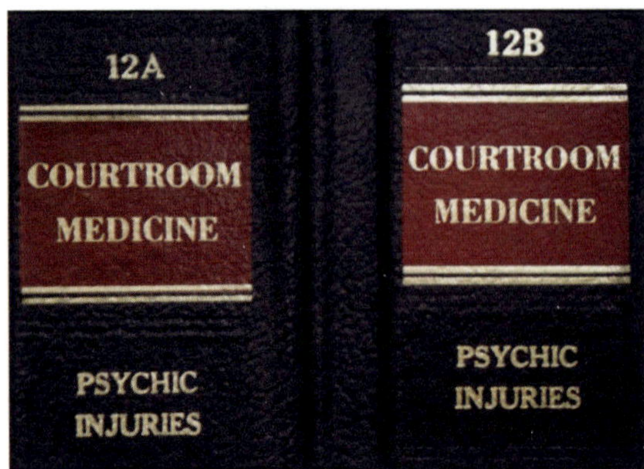

Psychic injuries.

THE

SELF-INFLICTED

WOUND

by Fred P. Graham

Book titles of the day. Law books are often a portal into a strange alternative universe.

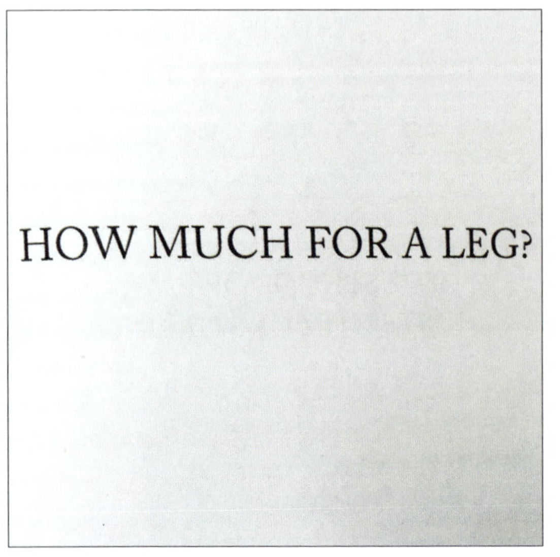

HOW MUCH FOR A LEG?

Law books have the best titles.

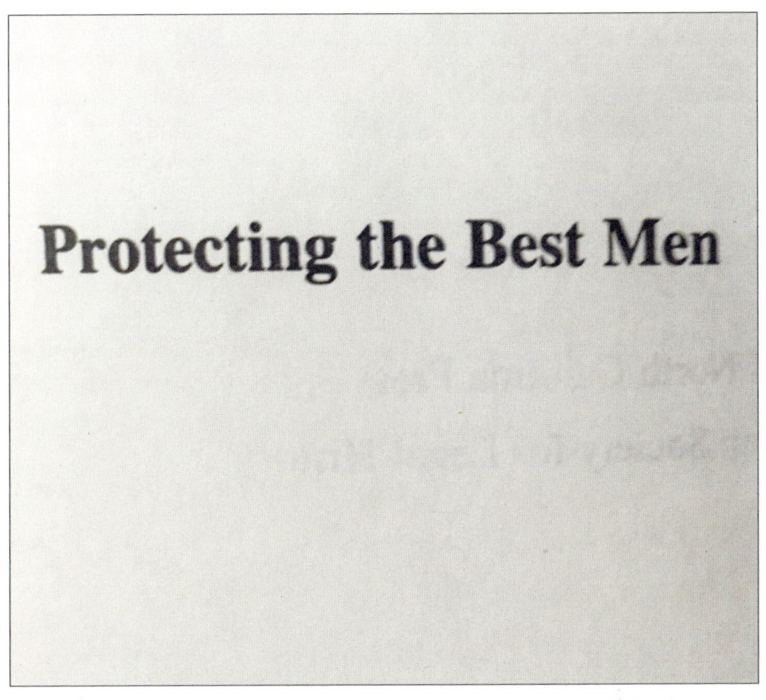
Protecting the Best Men

You have to admire the frank honesty of such a book title.

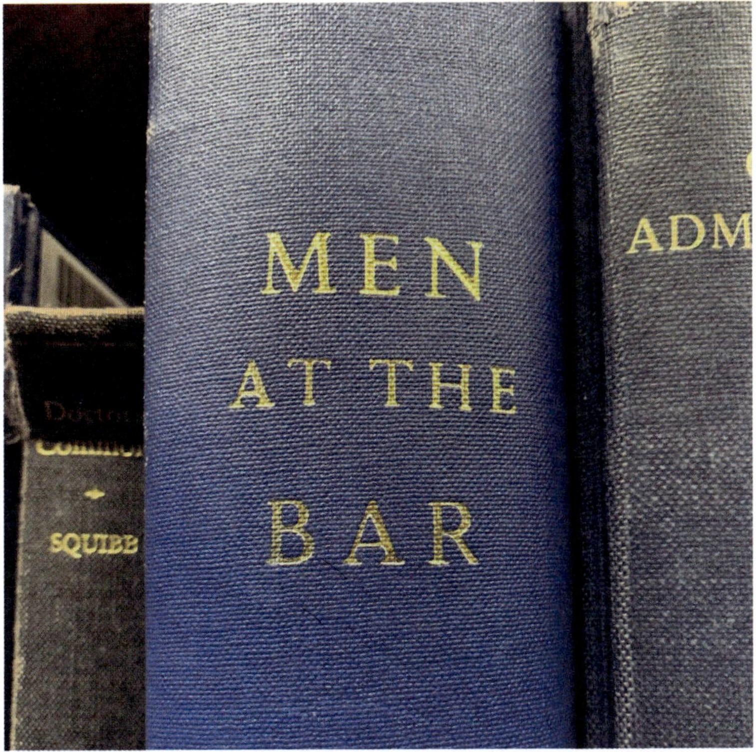

Bodleian Library, book title of the day.

LEMN SISSAY

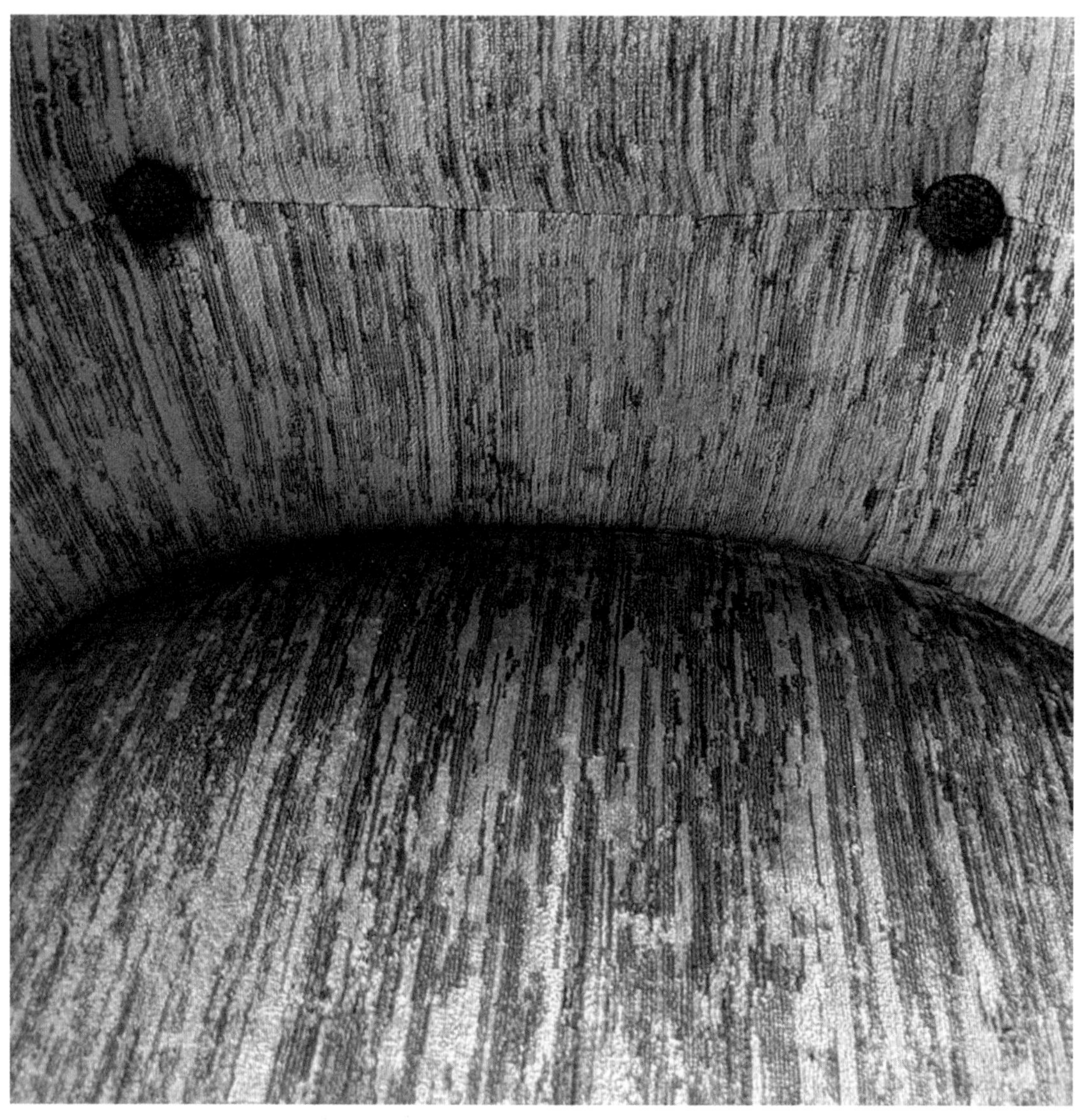

Throughout the night a hotel chair has been staring at me. But what is it thinking?

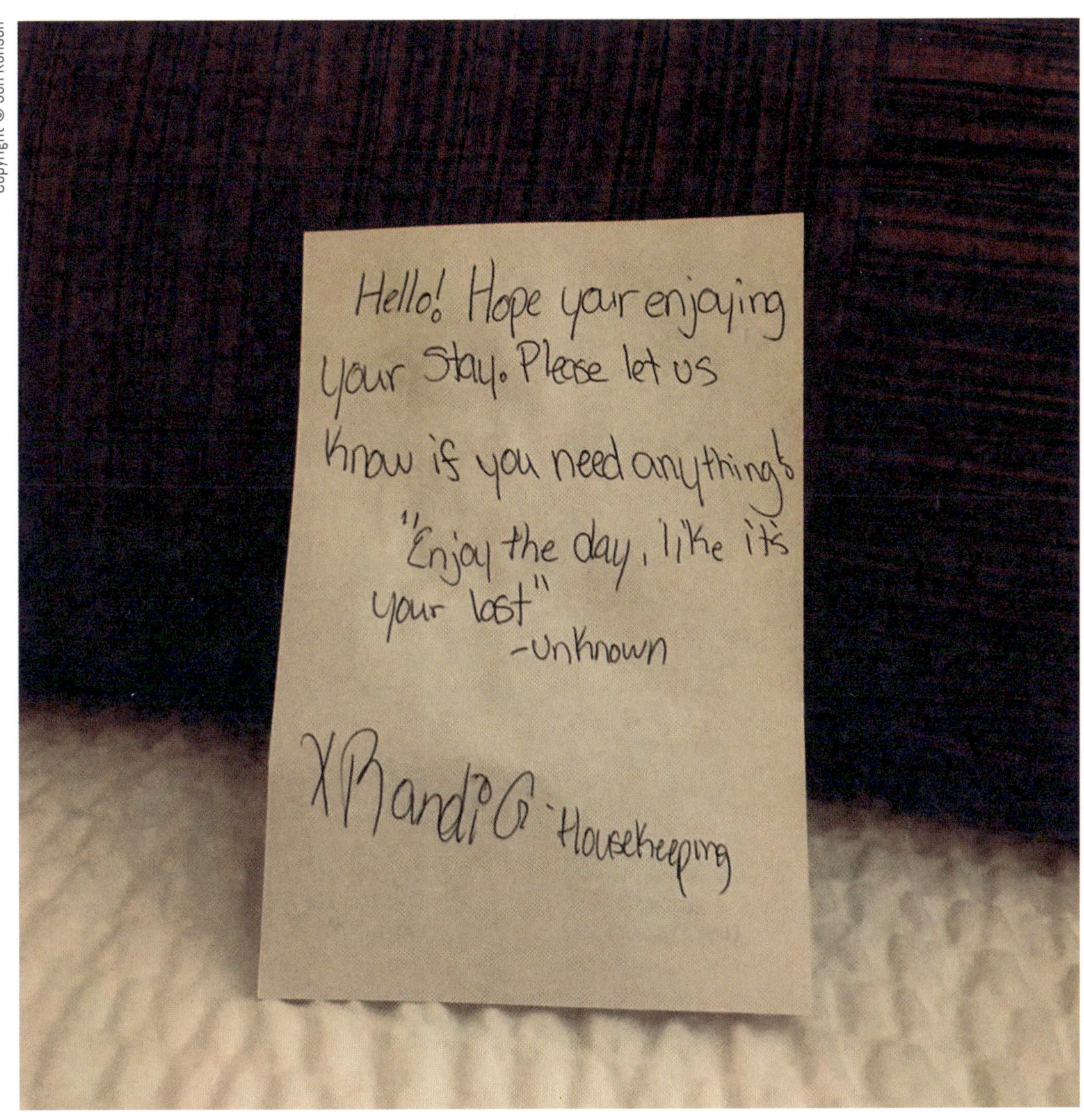

Lovely, then ominous.

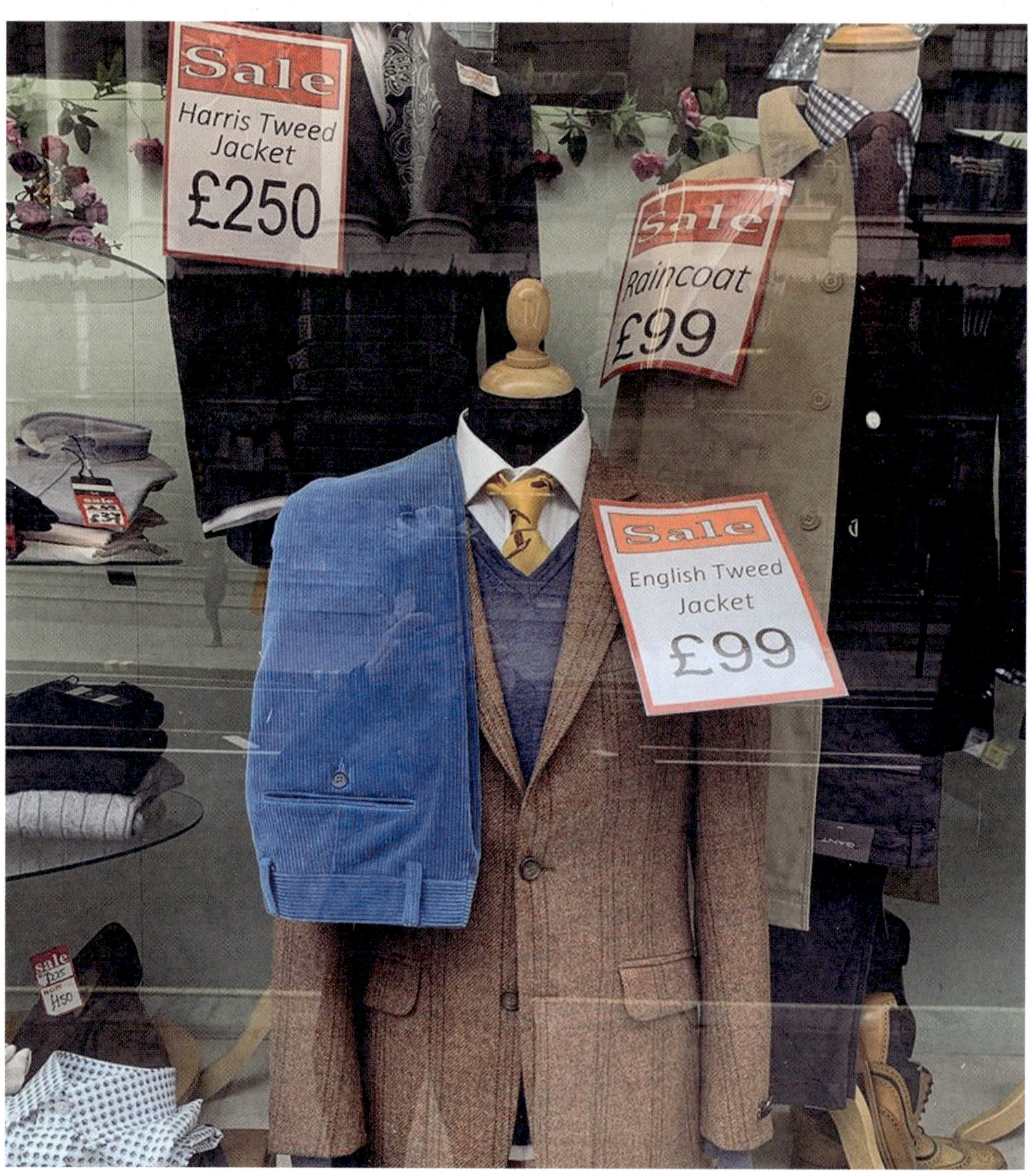

Aristo traditions.

THE POLITICIAN.

"A politician should (as I have read)
Be furnish'd in the first place with a head."

Hogarth.

RACHEL WHITEREAD

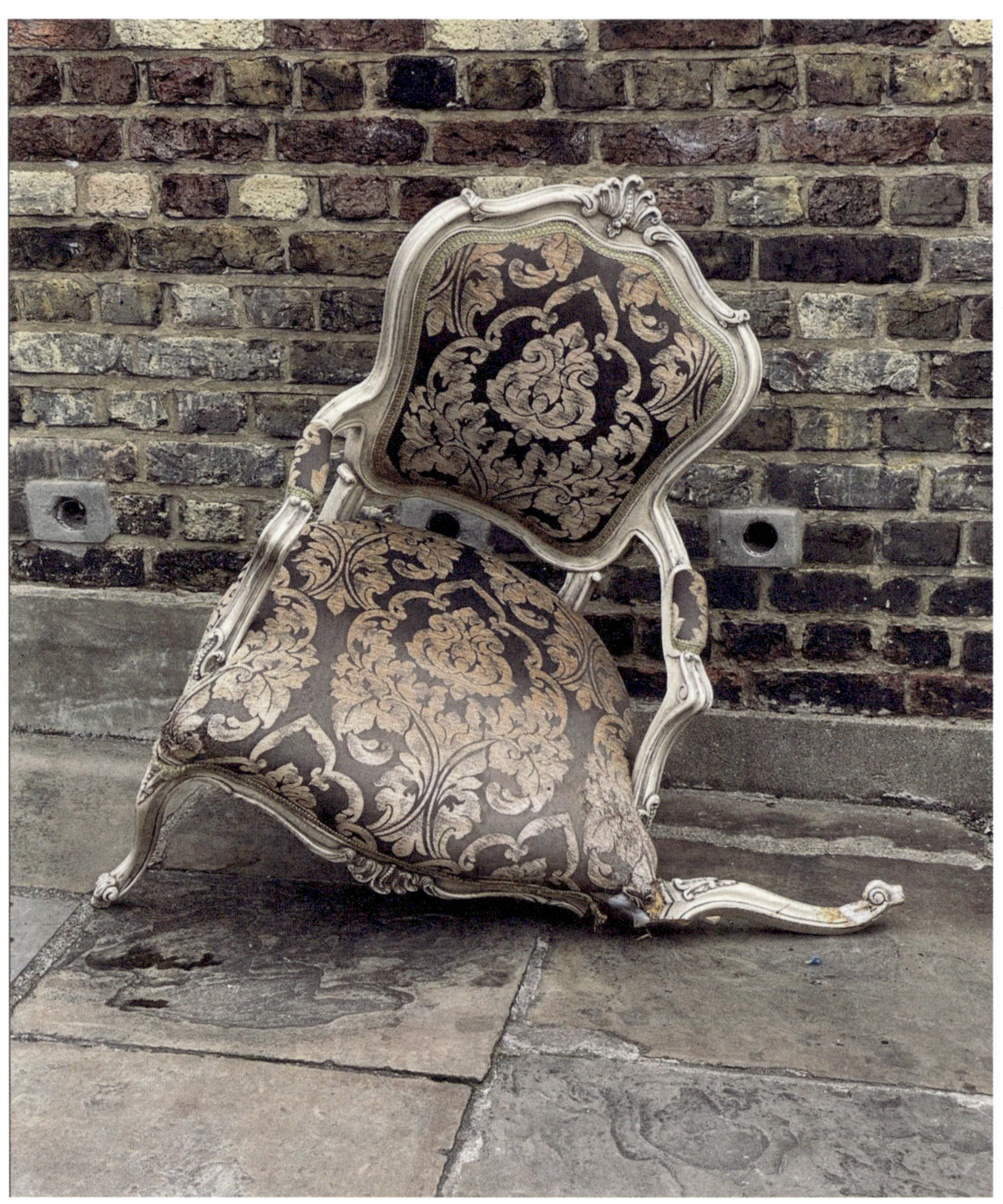

Currently recovering from a long overdue knee operation.

5: creative places

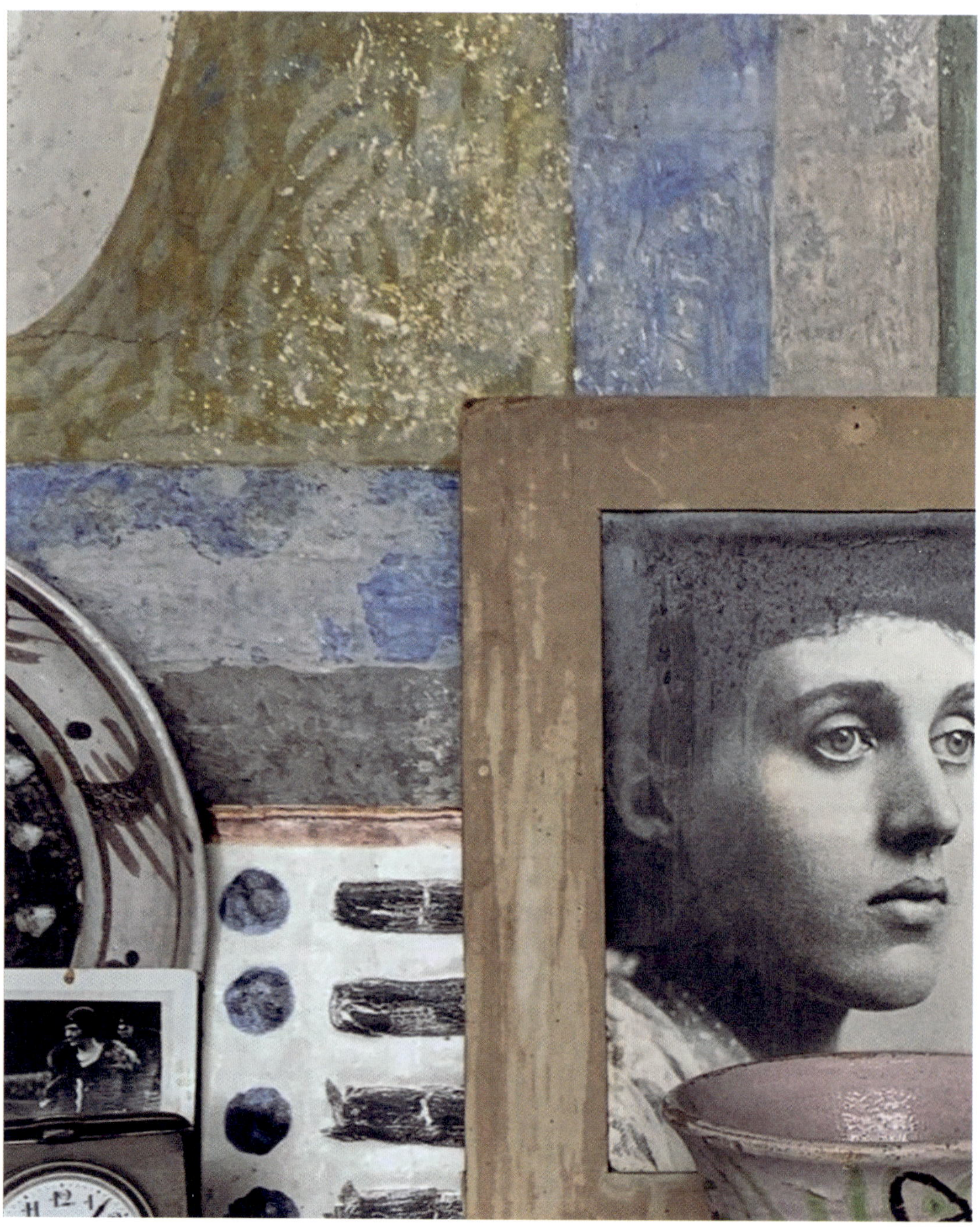

Thank you @charlestontrust.

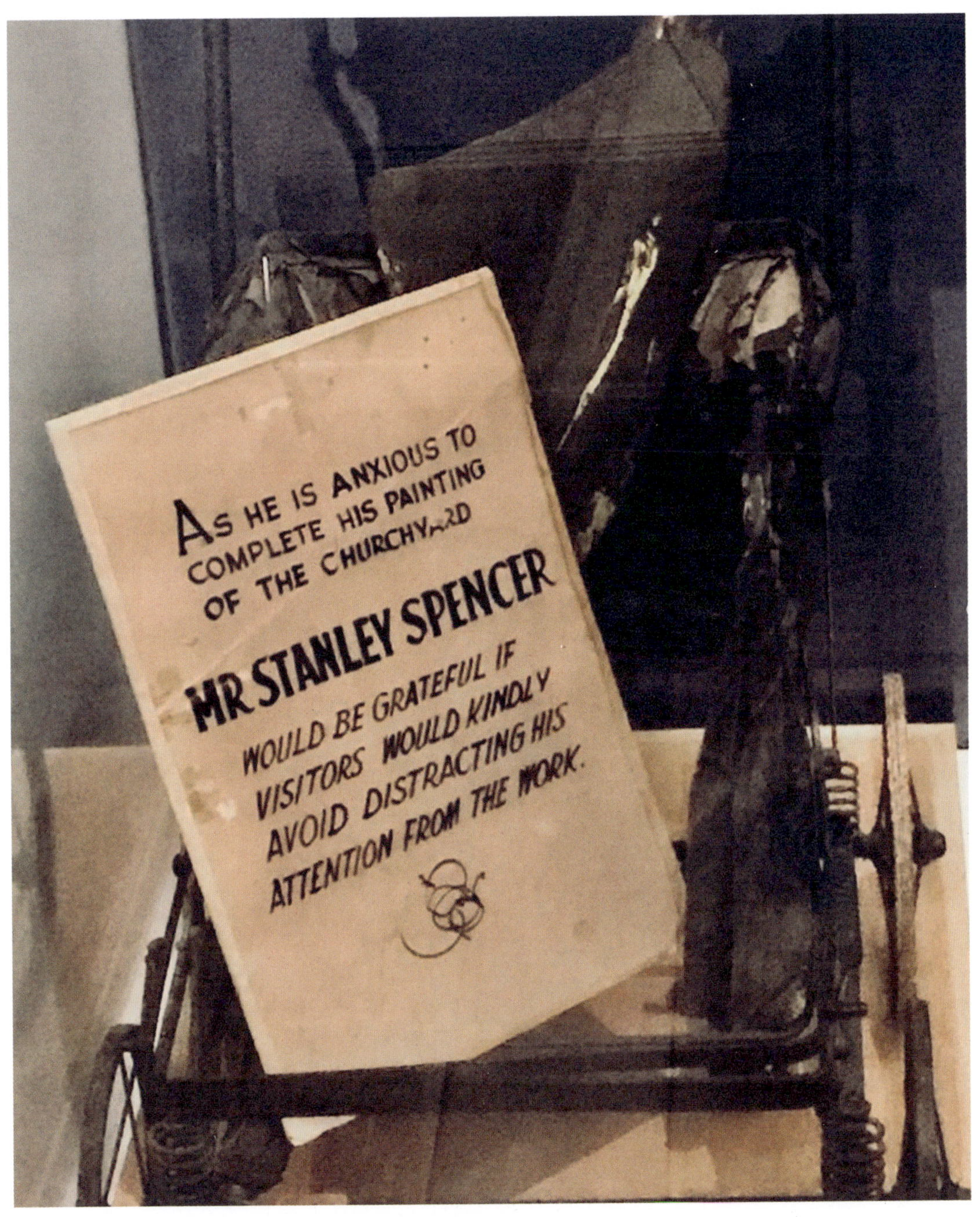

Stanley Spencer. 'I am on the side of angels and of dirt' (The sign is in his gallery in Cookham, which is just one and a half rooms and is exactly as sensational as you'd imagine).

ELIF SHAFAK

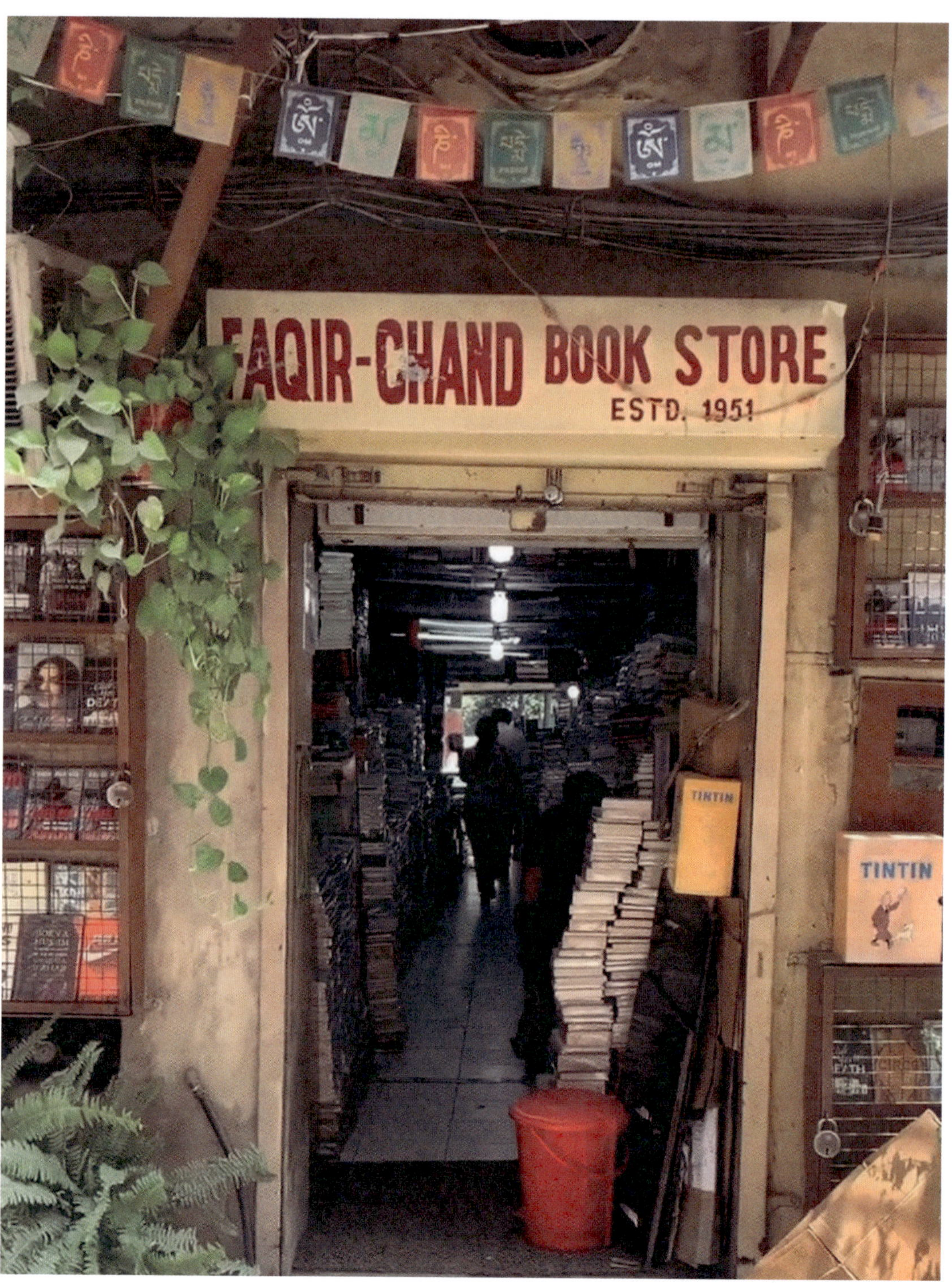

This will make you smile, the magical beauty of a bookstore.

A LOCAL SECOND-HAND BOOKSHOP has shelves labelled 'Cult': Burroughs, Bukowski, Anaïs Nin and the Marquis de Sade and books on witchcraft, Charles Manson and Jack the Ripper. We seekers after holy relics on dusty shelves are ourselves a cult, poking about among the ruins. In David Hare's film *Wetherby*, Marcia, a librarian, is driving with a friend to a jumble sale with boxes of second-hand clothes. The man expounds a theory – he's read it in a book – that 'murder is characteristically committed by people who handle other people's things. In second-hand clothes shops, junk shops, markets ... Self-improvement, that's another hallmark. People who teach themselves things, at home, at night...A fantasy life of singular intensity.' Marcia suggests that the man is keen on murder himself: 'Yes, oh God, yes, I'm addicted.' In turn, he asks, 'Do *you* like murder?' and Marcia replies: 'Not much. But I prefer it to romance.'

JARVIS COCKER

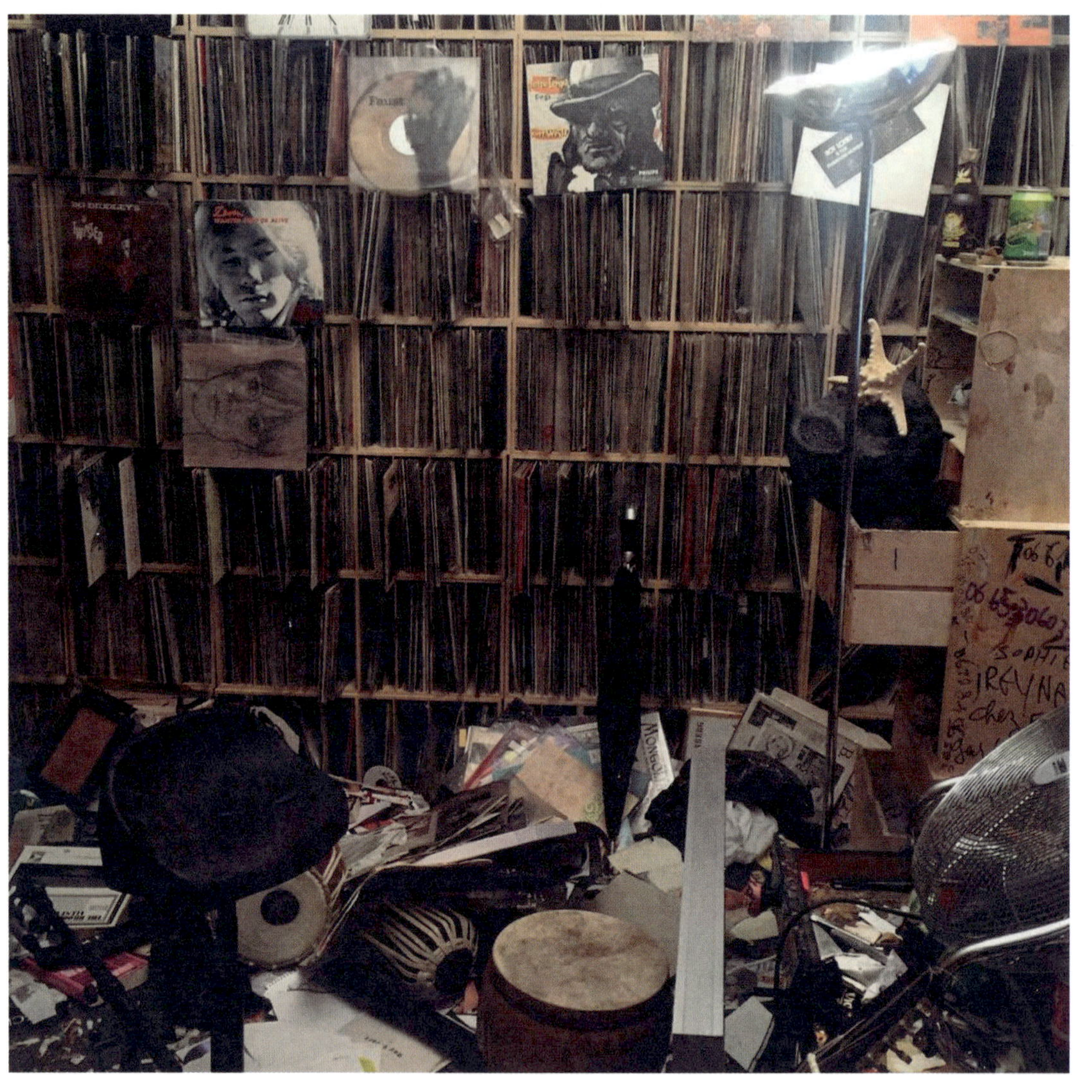

Just been tidying my room ... Only joking: this is an artwork called *La Pièce de Vie* by Robert Combas. It features in an exhibition by the author Michel Houellebecq.

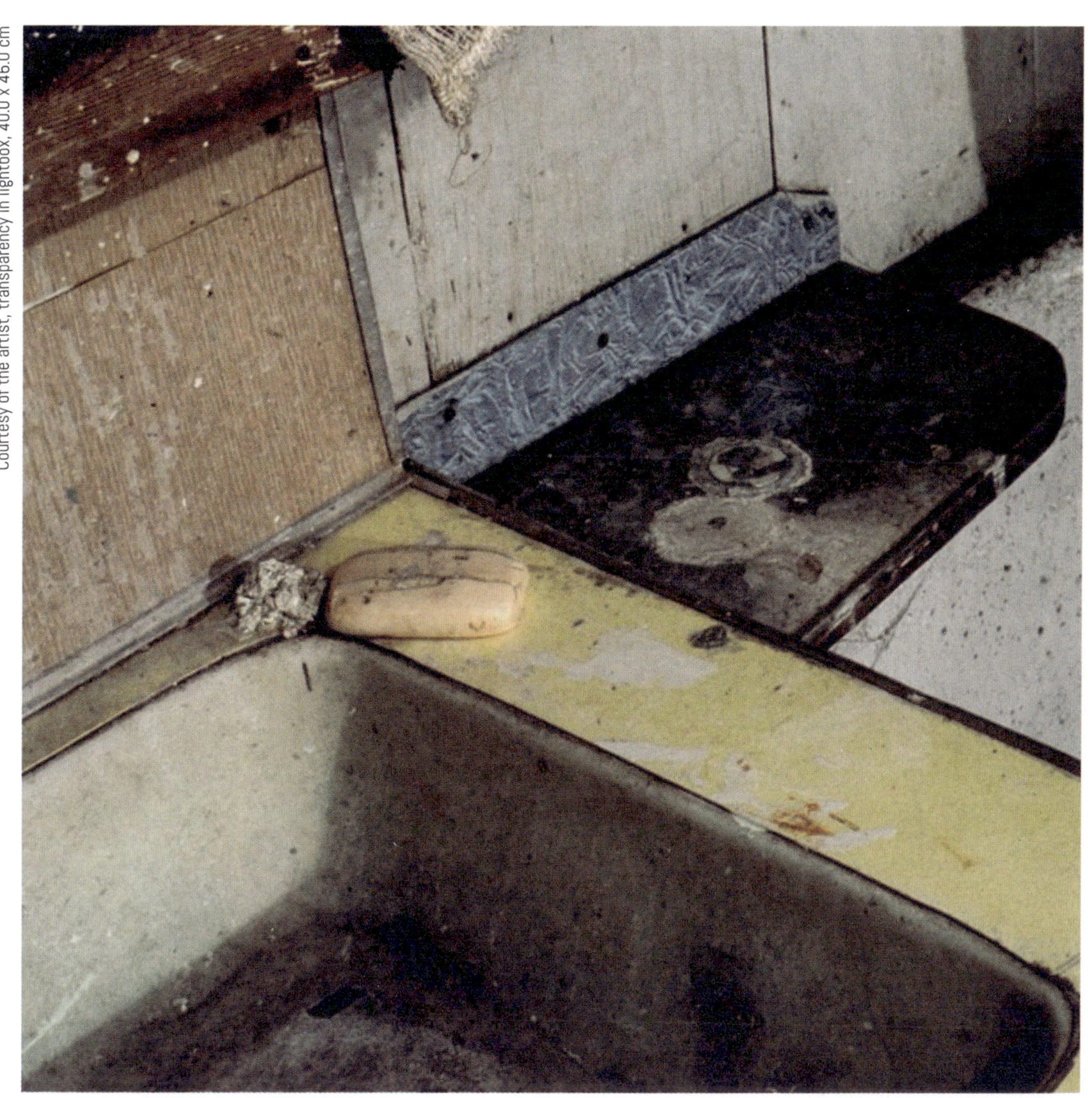

Courtesy of the artist, transparency in lightbox, 40.0 x 46.0 cm

Jeff Wall, *Diagonal composition*, 1993.

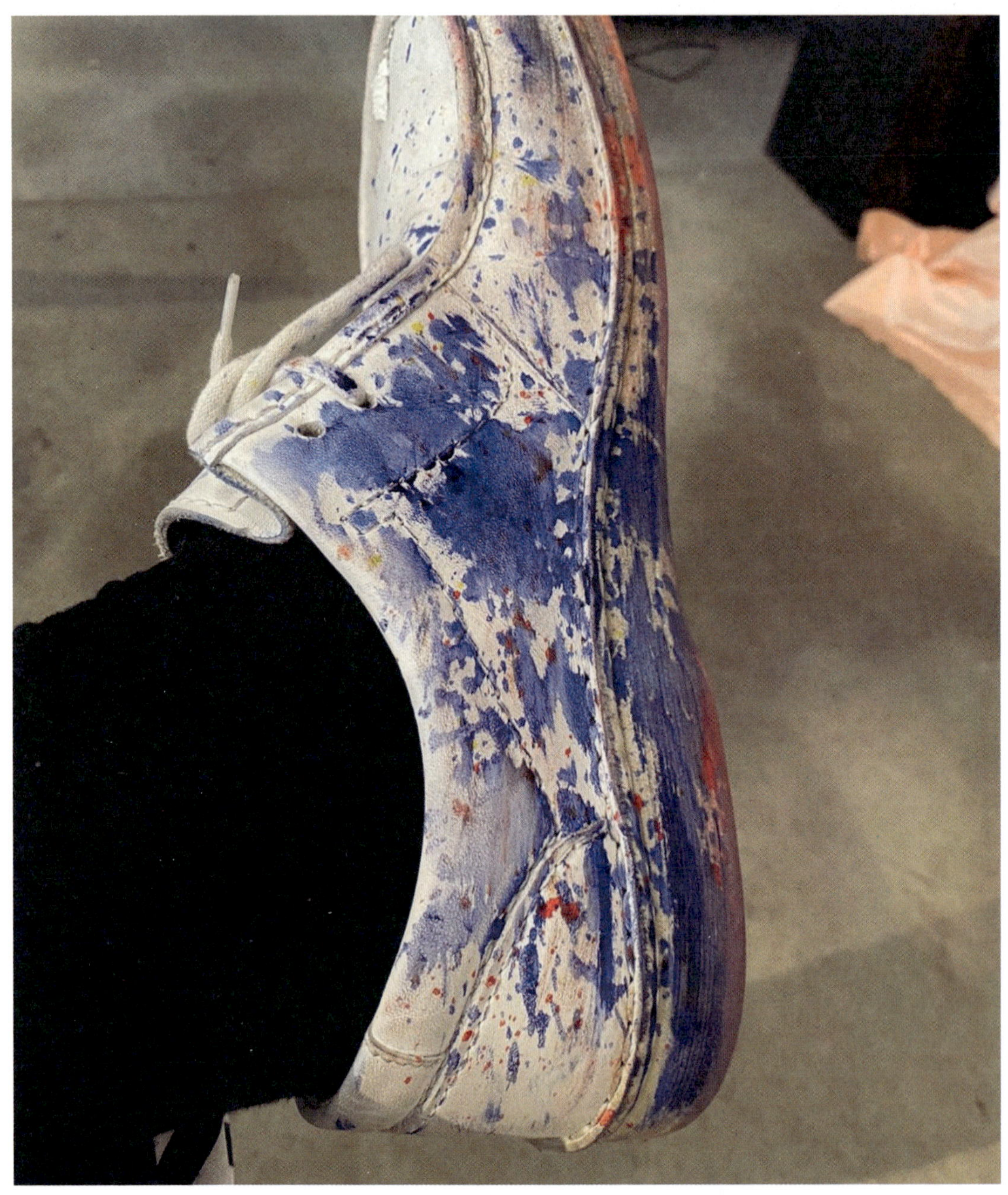

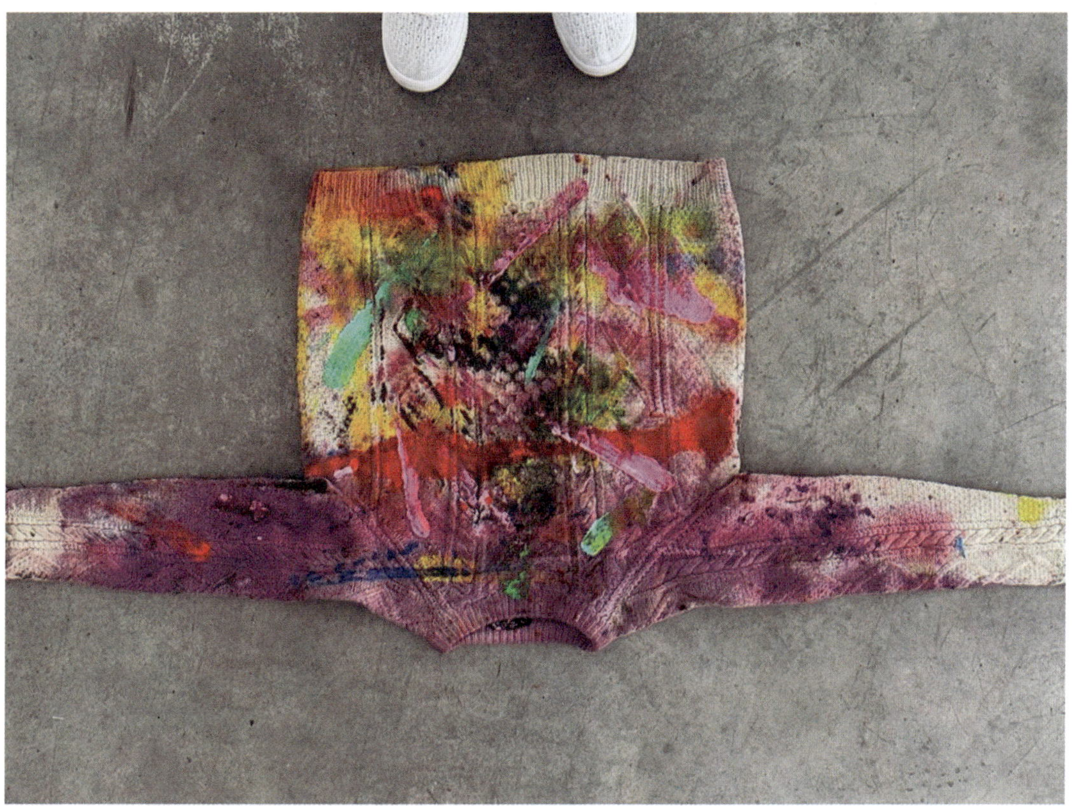

Studio sweater.

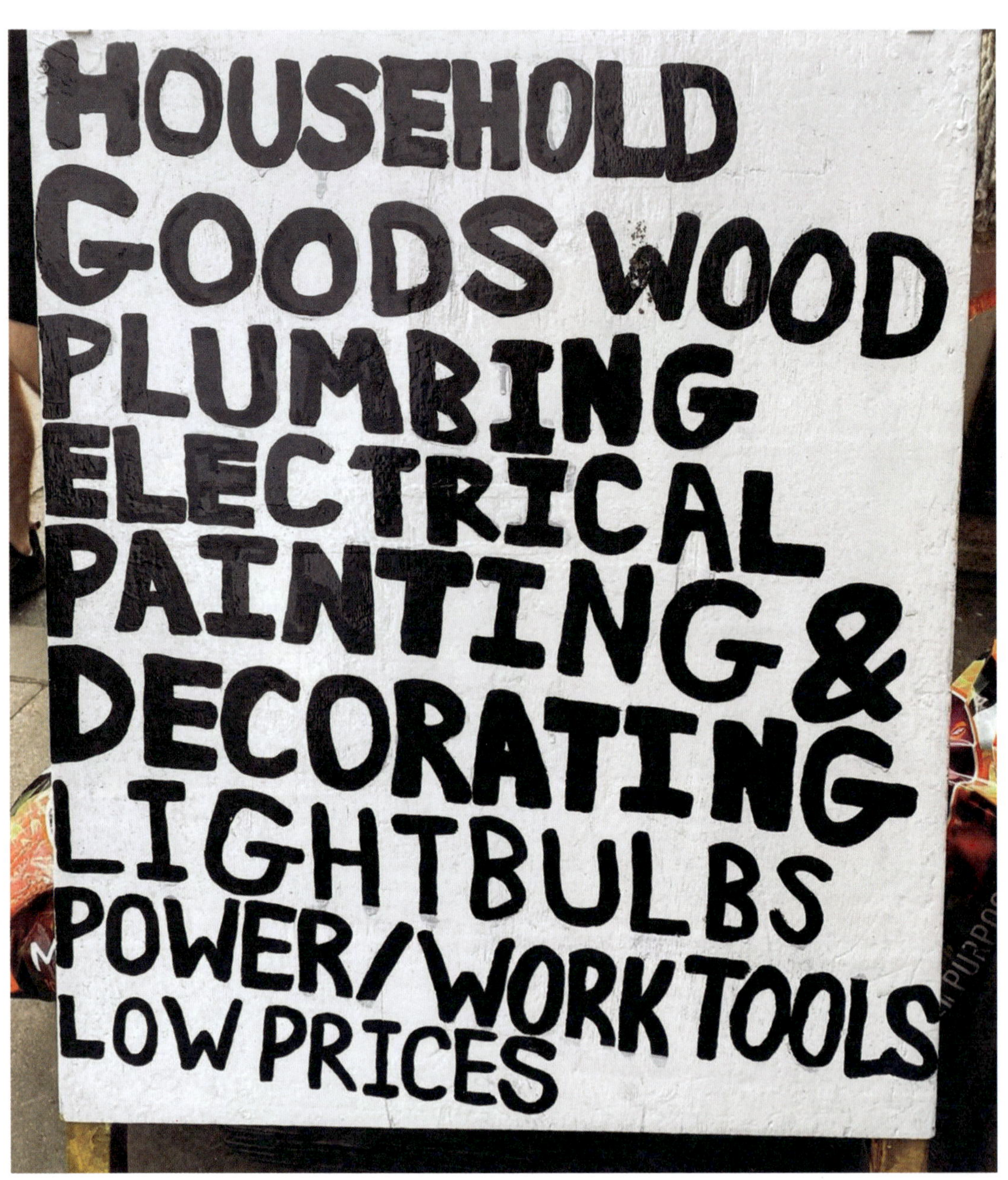

Studio materials ... sorted!

CORNELIA PARKER

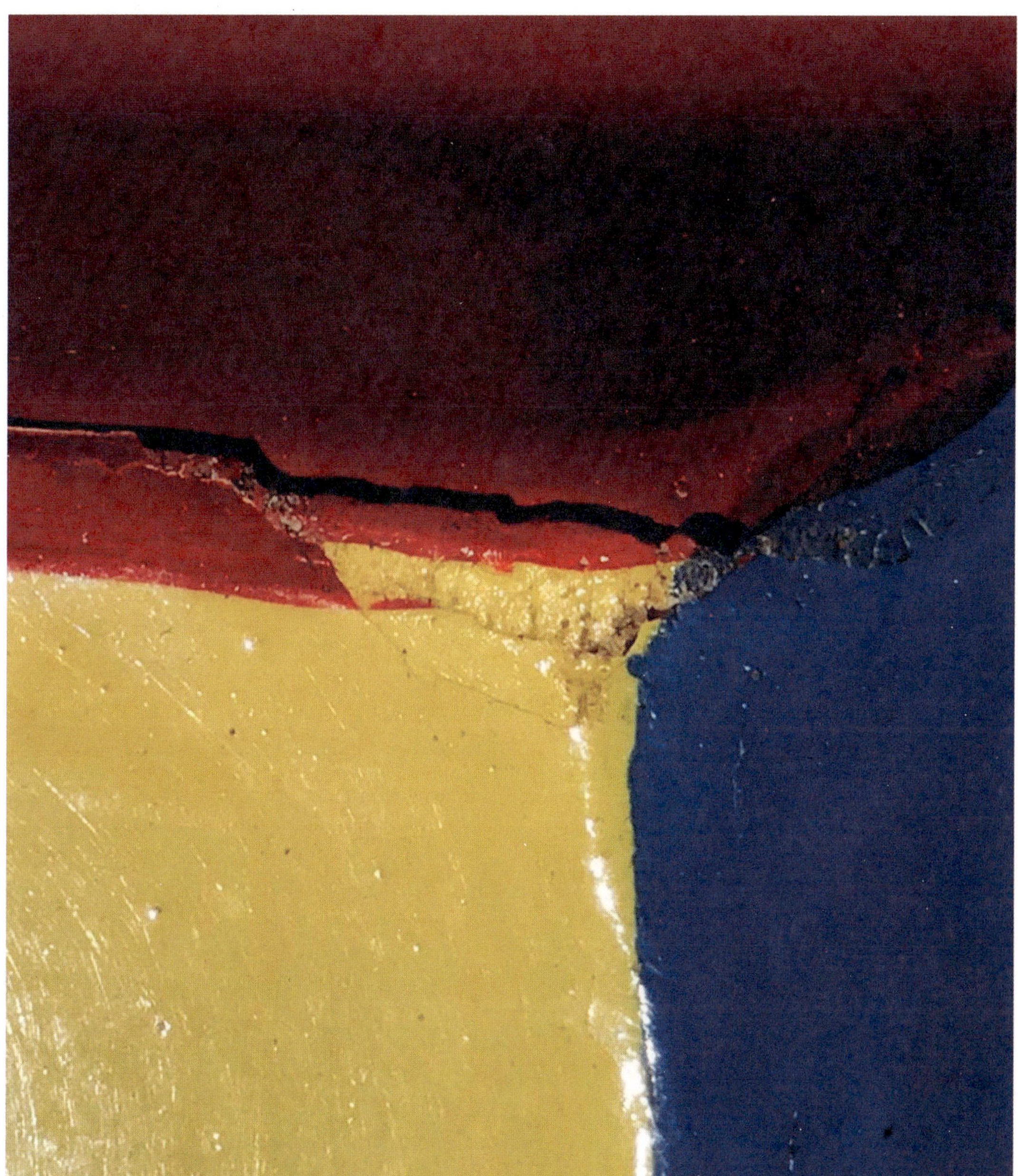

Cracks beginning to show.

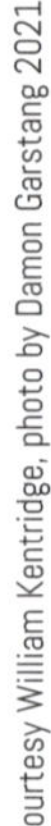

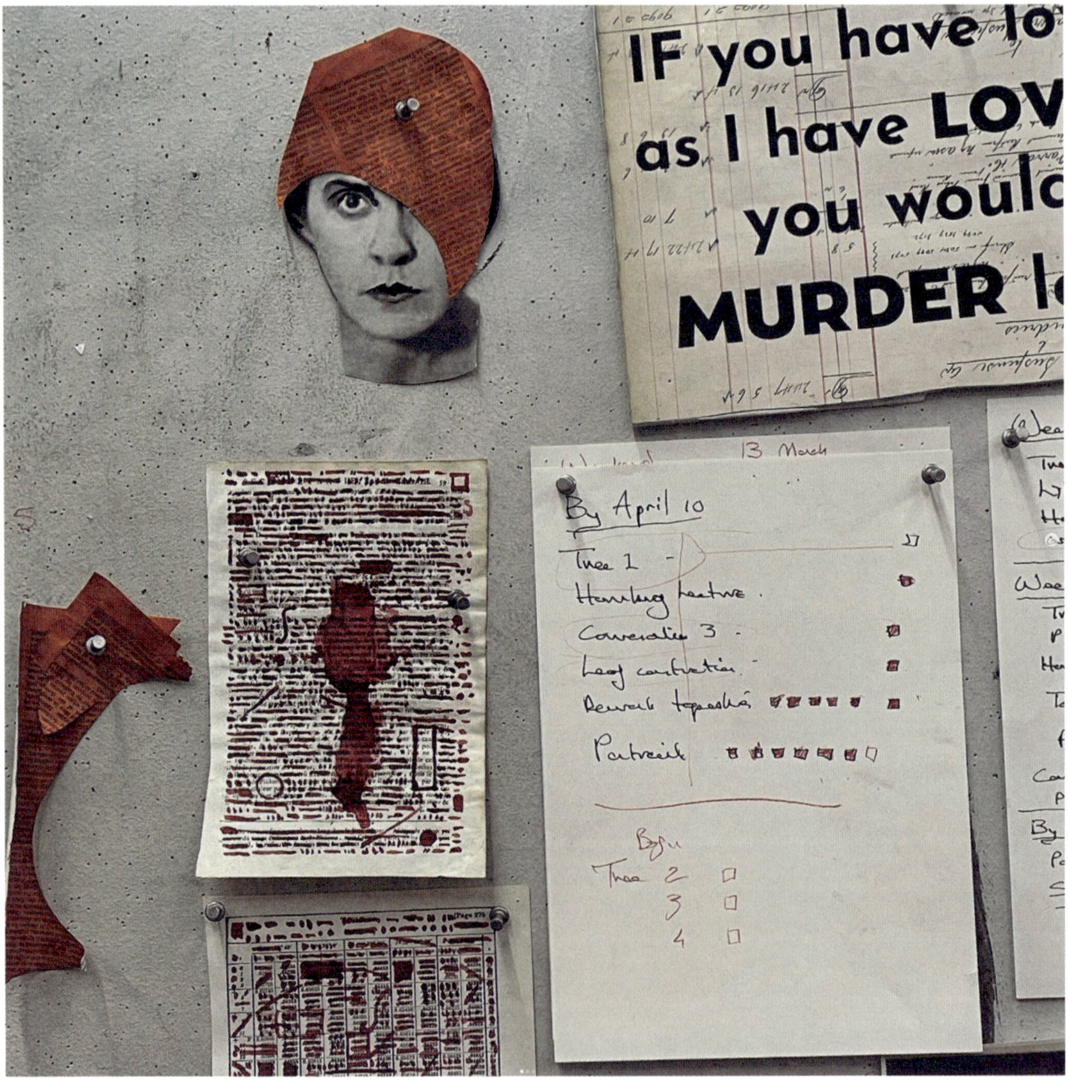

Courtesy William Kentridge, photo by Damon Garstang 2021

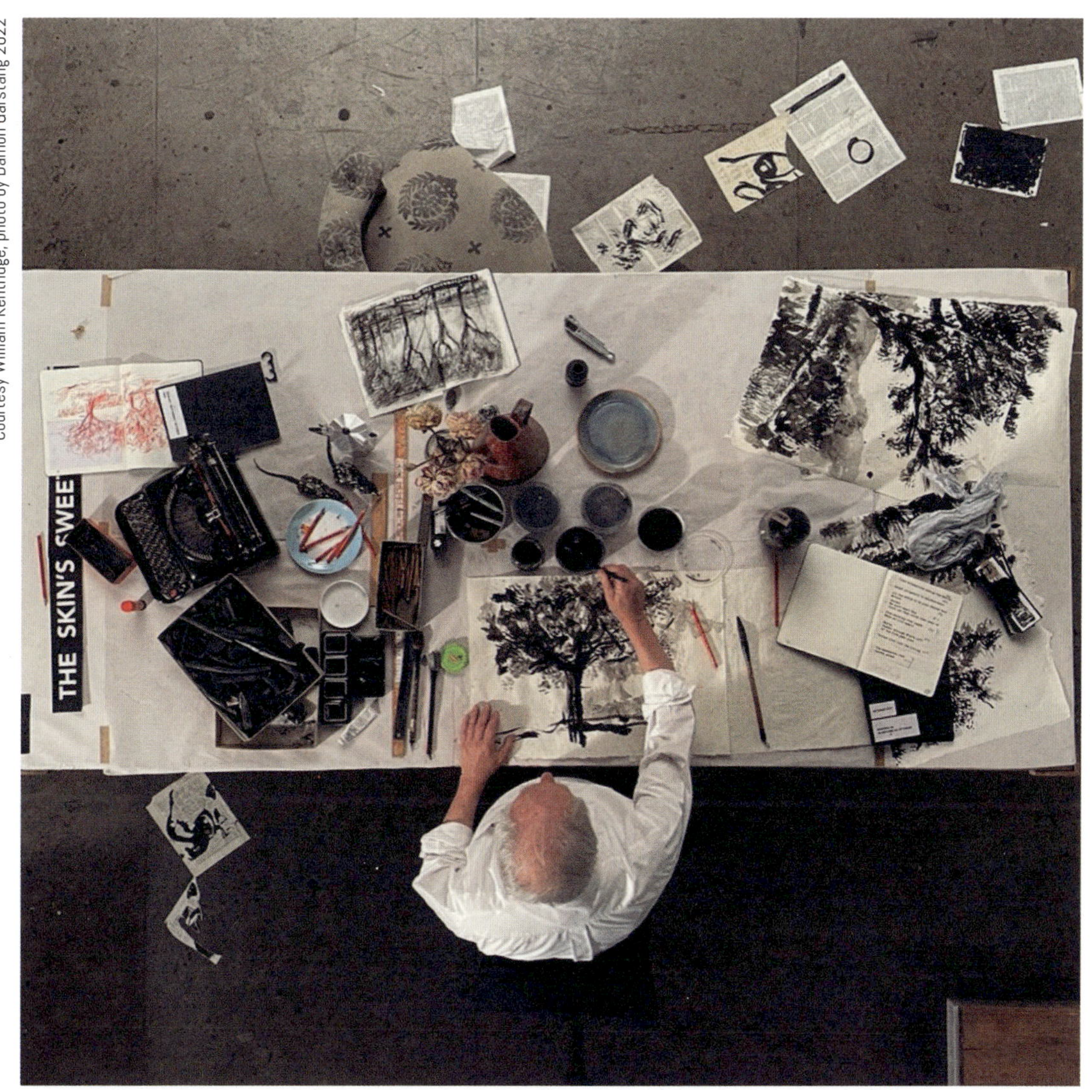

Courtesy William Kentridge, photo by Damon Garstang 2022

Silence reigns supreme.

PETER DOIG

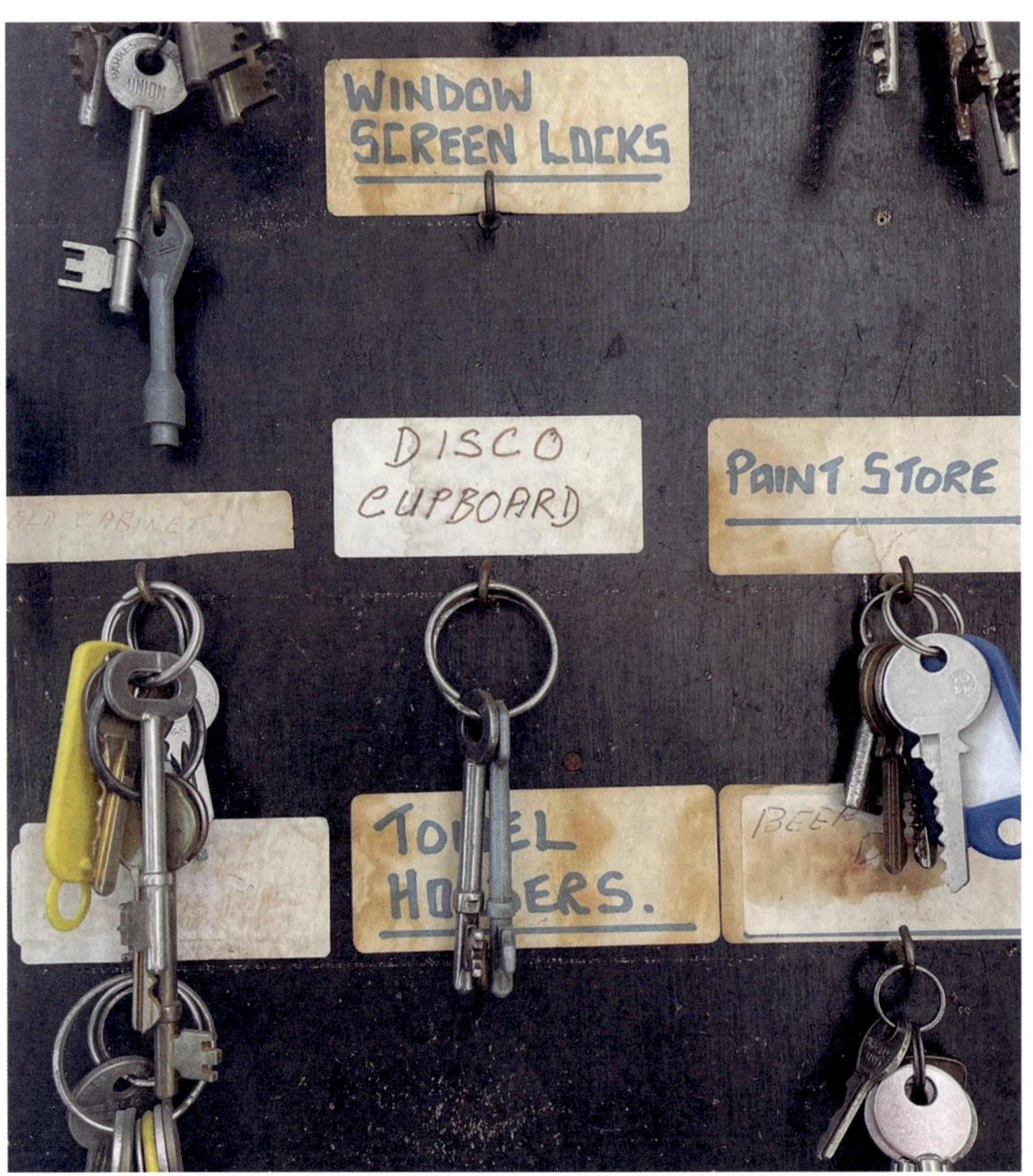

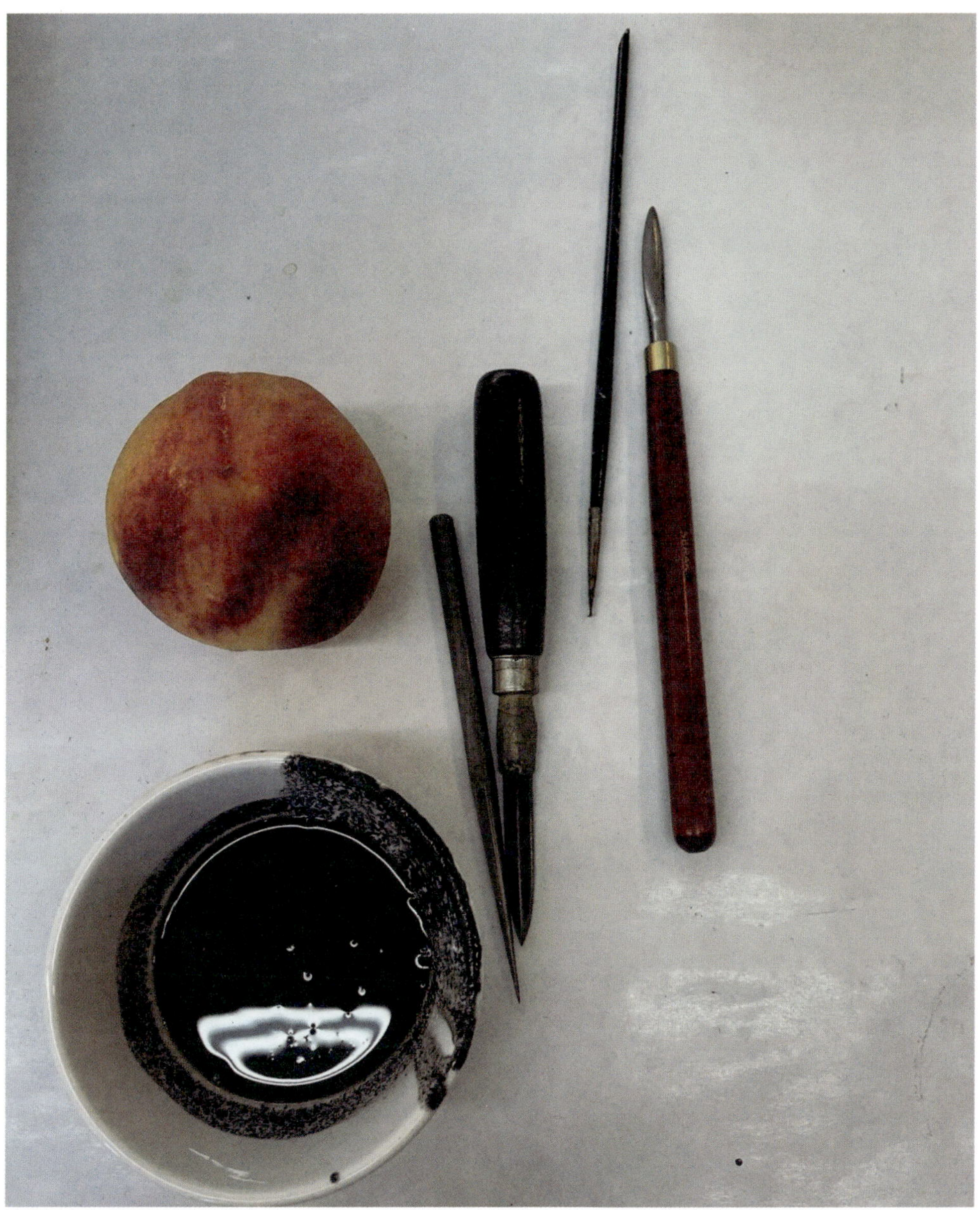

Etching again.

AVEEK SEN

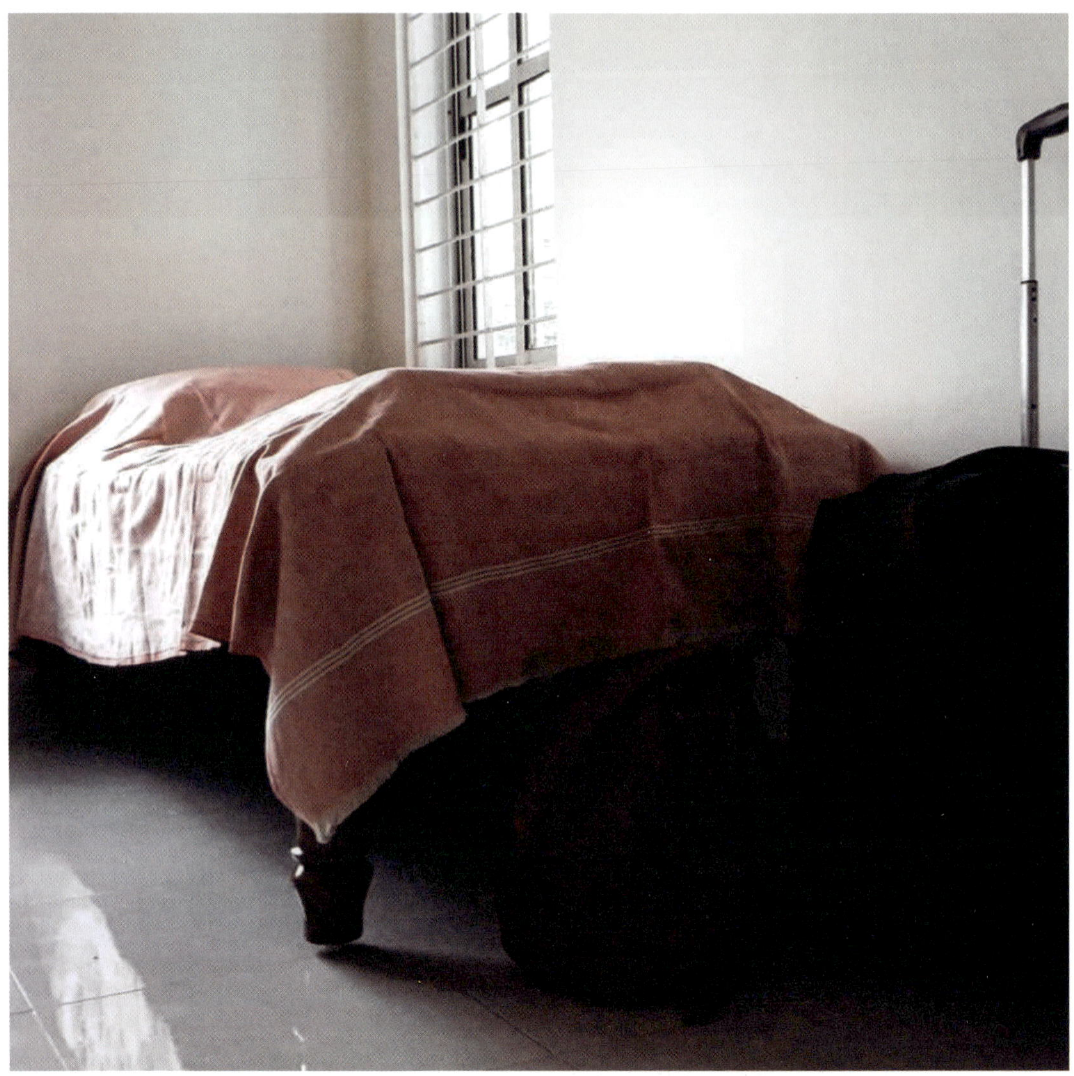

My home until mid-October. Bareness, quiet, light, birdsong, senior citizens and trees. Nothing on the walls. And an exquisitely narrow bed. One's inner nun is ecstatic.

First published in 2023
Redstone Press, 7a St Lawrence Terrace, London W10 5SU
email: redstone.press@gmail.com
website: www.theredstoneshop.com

ISBN 978-1-7395976-2-7

Design: Julian Rothenstein / Artwork: Tom Baxter
Production: Geoff Barlow / Manufacture:1010 Printing International Limited, China

Distributed worldwide excluding the UK by
Artbook I D.A.P.
75 Broad Street, Suite 630
New York, NY 10004
artbook.com

Thanks to: Salwa Benloubane, Anne Clarke, Sarmistha Das, Faith Evans, Leo Hollis, Natalie Hume, Hiang Kee, Elisa Nadel, Ella Rothenstein, Lucien Rothenstein, Ardu Vakil, Isabella Thomas, Mog Yoshihara.

* * *

CORNELIA PARKER, CBE, RA
is one of Britain's best loved and most acclaimed contemporary artists.

JULIAN ROTHENSTEIN
founded Redstone Press in 1986. He has edited and designed many books, most recently *Everyday Play: A Campaign Against Boredom* and *A Gift (from Artists, Poets and Photographers under 13)*.
The celebrated annual *Redstone Diary*, is now in its 36th edition.
Books can be ordered from www.theredstoneshop.com

CHARLES BOYLE
has published poetry, fiction and non-fiction under his own name and two pen names.
In 2007 he founded the award-winning small press CB editions which has published over 70 titles, mostly short fiction and poetry, including work in translation.
Books can be ordered from www.cbeditions.com